THE Freedom TO *LOVE* AND *LIVE* Again

FORGIVENESS MADE POSSIBLE

Compiled By

DAVID E. RITZENTHALER

ISBN 0-7392-0122-0
Library of Congress Catalog Card Number 99-93630

Printed in the USA by

MORRIS PUBLISHING

3212 East Highway 30 • Kearney, NE 68847 • 1-800-650-7888

Authorship of This Book

Parts of the chapters in this book were written by the actual people whose life stories are being shared. Others were written by staff members at Victorious Christian Living, International (VCLI), a Christian discipleship organization. They drew from their personal experiences and their knowledge as disciples to convey the principles taught herein. My job was compiling these wonderful lessons, taught by the Holy Spirit, and arranging them into a sequence that would facilitate your understanding and application of these truths in your own life.

I wish to thank the Lord for blessing me with the privilege of watching His hand save so many lives from seemingly unrecoverable destruction. Thanks as well to all those who told their stories of God's touch upon their lives.

Because of Jesus,
David E. Ritzenthaler

Acknowledgements

This book was a team project. Without the coordination and direction of Rocky Nystrom, I would not have finished this book for publication. Thank you to Mark Ford and Ted Sellers who helped me finish writing. Brian Cabral, with his genius in editing and creative thought, made it possible for readers to understand what I intend to be understood. Kym Varner, my administrative assistant, has gone beyond the call of duty, sometimes working throughout the night to edit and rearrange chapters and thoughts. Without her, we could not have accomplished this project.

I want to recognize my parents who gave me the best child raising, spiritual heritage, and preparation to live in this world. My wife, Suzanne, and daughters, Tamara and Michele, continue to be my inspiration as I tried out what I was learning on them.

This project would not have been possible without the people in this book who shared their life stories with humility and openness.

Most of all, I want to thank my incredible Savior and Lord, Jesus Christ; my loving heavenly Father; and the empowering of the Holy Spirit for this supernatural Christian life.

David E. Ritzenthaler

Table of Contents

Introduction

Are you a person who has been badly wounded in relationships? Do you find yourself frustrated by longstanding wounds which adversely affect new relationships? Are you torn between wanting to be isolated from people to avoid being hurt again, yet hating the loneliness which is the price of safety?

Wounded people often construct their own prison to be safe. They construct the bars of anger, fear, frustration, distrust, and revenge. While they enjoy the safety, they find they are unable to function as a person.

If you are imprisoned, the keys to victory dangle in the lock of unforgiveness. Would you like to have the keys to open your prison, and a suit of armor to protect you from more wounds so you can leave the prison and still be safe? God has provided all this and more.

This book will teach you concepts of how to be free from the bondage of wounds and unforgiveness. You will also read the accounts of unimaginable atrocities and how the victims found total freedom through a relationship with Jesus Christ. God gives beauty for ashes, freedom for bondage. He is waiting to make your life new.

It is also written for those who have caused wounds in others, and now need guidance for restoring their relationship to God and rebuilding relationships with those they have hurt. Husbands or wives who have committed adultery will find this book particularly helpful. Parents who are interested in rebuilding relationships with their children will gain the tools to do that. Wounds to friends, co-workers and others in every day life can be healed because of the message in this book. The principles herein will help restore any relationship.

I dedicate this book to Jesus, the greatest forgiver, who led the way of forgiveness and provides the resources we need to forgive "as Jesus forgave."

Because of Jesus,
David E. Ritzenthaler

Chapter One

Freedom to Love and Live Again

Are you living unnecessarily in condemnation, shame, or anxiety because you feel unforgiven or even unforgivable? Are you imprisoned by bitterness, anger, or resentment because of what others have done to you? Have you caused hurt and pain in someone else's life, and now live in bondage to the torment of guilt? Is there unresolved strife between you and family members, friends, or co-workers causing gnawing tension? The Lord Jesus came to set you free! You can be free to love and live again <u>if</u> you warmly embrace God's principles of forgiveness.

This is not a book about methods or "how to's." It is about the wonderful, supernatural life of Christ who enables you to love and live again through forgiveness and reconciliation. Though steps of forgiveness are a tool we use, they are not the end all. Without the dynamic, supernatural life of Christ as your experience, even the best described steps will not produce reconciliation. Thus, dependence should be placed in the person of Jesus Christ, not on a set of steps that lead to forgiveness.

There are four basic parts to forgiveness:
1. Christ's total forgiveness of you as a believer.
2. Giving forgiveness to those who have wounded or hurt you.
3. Seeking forgiveness from those you have wronged or hurt.
4. Rebuilding broken relationships in the love of Christ.

PART ONE: CHRIST FORGIVES YOU

Only by accepting Christ and realizing the impact <u>His</u> forgiveness has on your life, will you be able to forgive others, seek other's forgiveness, and rebuild your broken relationships. Believing in and trusting the love and forgiveness of Jesus Christ is the bedrock on which to begin loving and living again. *For God so* loved the world, that He gave His only begotten Son, that whoever believes in Him should not perish, but have eternal life (John 3:16). In this is love, not that we loved God, but that He loved us and sent His Son to be the propitiation for our sins (1 John 4:10).

Do you experience the depth of God's love and forgiveness of you?

PART TWO: GIVING FORGIVENESS

The second part of forgiveness is giving forgiveness to those who have wronged you. *And be kind to one another, tender-hearted, forgiving each other, just as God in Christ also has forgiven you* (Ephesians 4:32). How did Jesus forgive you? By no longer holding you responsible to "pay the price" for sin. You are commanded by Christ to give the same forgiveness to others.

All of us have seen families torn apart because someone will not forgive or does not know how to forgive. A high percentage of marriages end unnecessarily in divorce because one partner cannot forgive the other. Even churches often fail to represent the Gospel of Jesus Christ, split asunder by relationships where forgiveness is needed but not given. Entire nations live with constant civil war because of "unforgiveness." Forgiveness is one of the greatest needs of mankind.

Giving forgiveness is something people know they need to do, but they often don't know how. People often say they forgive, but actually experience very little or none of the freedom that comes from true forgiveness. What many do in the name of forgiveness isn't forgiveness at all. They don't take the steps necessary to truly give forgiveness and then experience the real freedom and the ability to love that comes from that forgiveness.

After years of counseling people who need to give forgiveness, I am convinced that there are simple steps you can take to experience the freedom and ability to love those who hurt you. But first you must understand the barriers that stand in the way of truly giving forgiveness.

The greatest barrier to forgiveness is that the offended person is fearful of being hurt again. They fear that, if they make themselves "vulnerable" by forgiving the offender, the offender will take advantage of their weakness and will hurt them again. As you read

2

Chapter Seven, you will discover how Lisa received the power to become vulnerable to her offender without being hurt again.

Another common barrier to forgiveness is that the "offended" person simply does not want to forgive. They relish the power that withholding forgiveness gives them over the offender. They are "playing god."

The third reason is that most of us simply don't know how to give forgiveness correctly. No one has taught us the actual, practical steps to giving forgiveness. Most of us have been told to forgive but have never experienced the practical, day-to-day working out of the supernatural life of Christ.

The fourth barrier is that we are lacking the power to forgive anyone. Even if we actually know how and know that we should give forgiveness, we don't have the ability to do so.

Would you like to be set free from the prison of unforgiveness, and rid yourself of the torment of bitterness, resentment, or anger? The chapters that follow will show you how.

PART THREE: SEEKING FORGIVENESS

Seeking forgiveness from those you have wronged is essential to experiencing the freedom to love and live again. Yet, it is one of the most commonly neglected commands that God gives us. *"If therefore you are presenting your offering at the altar, and there remember that your brother* <u>*has something against you,*</u> *leave your offering there before the altar, and go your way; first be reconciled to your brother, and then come and present your offering"* (Matthew 5:23-24, emphasis added). Seeking forgiveness means humbling one's self in admission of wrong, and asking to be released from the responsibility of sin committed against someone.

Many Christians balk at that principle. Most simply refuse to humble themselves and admit that they were wrong. Others don't know how to accomplish what the Lord commands them to do. Less mature believers don't even know the Lord has put the ball in their court.

As long as we live on this earth, in these human bodies, we will be prone to offend other people. Those offenses may be blatant or subtle, large or small. Regardless, the Lord commands us to "be reconciled," to acknowledge our wrongs toward others, and seek their forgiveness.

If you are trapped by guilt and shame because of something you have said or done to hurt someone, there is hope. We will show you simple steps you can take to seek forgiveness.

PART FOUR: REBUILDING RELATIONSHIPS

Rebuilding relationships is the crown jewel of complete forgiveness. It requires reconciliation and the willingness to love others with the love of Jesus Christ. Once a person begins to experience God's love and forgiveness, they are set free to "pour out" that love by giving forgiveness to those who have wronged them and seeking forgiveness from those they have wronged. Then broken relationships can be rebuilt.

During my years in ministry, helping others to put their lives back together, I have noticed an interesting phenomenon. No one has ever told me that they <u>don't</u> want to be free from bondage. But when it comes to following the simple steps that will free them from bondage, not everyone is willing.

Most will agree on the need for all four parts of forgiveness. Almost everyone gets excited about experiencing God's forgiveness of them. Some comply with God's command to give forgiveness. A few will even admit they have wronged others, and will seek forgiveness from them. However, only a very select few will follow through to the logical conclusion of forgiveness: rebuilding relationships.

"I can forgive that person," they say, "but I don't want to have anything to do with them." And yet, they insist that they want to be free from their bondage! What happened?

One hindrance to total forgiveness is evident every time a person does not follow through to the end: PRIDE. It is pride that keeps a person from experiencing God's love. It is greater pride that keeps someone from giving forgiveness. Still greater pride stops a person from seeking forgiveness. The ultimate pride denies restoration of relationships.

Have you followed through on all of which God has convicted you? Perhaps you would like to rebuild an important relationship in your life. If so, keep that relationship in mind and read on and you will see how to be set free to love and live again.

The purpose of this book is to give you the tools, examples, illustrations, and insight to understand what prevents you from experiencing every part of forgiveness. We will give you the knowledge you need in order to truly live in God's forgiveness, give forgiveness, seek forgiveness, and rebuild broken relationships.

This book is not a theological discussion of words in Scripture, but rather a practical manual on how to enjoy the freedom and benefits that come from experiencing God's forgiveness, giving forgiveness, seeking forgiveness, and being restored in relationships. All these are possible only with the resources available through Jesus, the Lord of Lords and King of Kings.

Testimonies in this book recount stories from real peoples' lives, in raw, uncensored form. I have asked them to share these powerful experiences to illustrate how true forgiveness works. These are not fictional stories. They are factual, first-hand accounts of tragedy, complete forgiveness, and the liberating results of forgiveness granted on God's terms and by His power.

Though we hear these kinds of stories (and worse) daily in our ministry to people, some of the stories, because of content, may be difficult to read. But I believe their details will convince you of the gravity and depth of the wounds and the magnitude of the forgiveness required. Perhaps these stories will help you to realize that there is hope, regardless of how impossible or tragic your situation seems. God writes openly and honestly in His Word about the depravity of even His own servants. God doesn't "sugarcoat" the realities of life.

These stories, and the lessons we take from them, will show the possibilities, and the powerful magnitude, of true forgiveness. Because of Jesus, and only because of Him, these stories of forgiveness are possible. These people were able to forgive "as Jesus forgave." He asks the impossible, and makes it possible. Jesus, who did not need to forgive and did nothing to be forgiven for, becomes not only the greatest example of forgiveness, but provides the possibility and the ability to forgive. Anyone who lives in the torment of life's experiences and wants to be free can be free indeed.

The Freedom to Love and Live Again

In the next few pages, these incredible yet simple truths will be displayed, taught, and explained through the lives of ordinary people who have lived through tragic life experiences. They will show you how they went from bondage to freedom, with the ability to love and live again.

By following these simple steps and practical demonstrations, you can learn to truly forgive and be released from the prison of unforgiveness. I trust these examples from the lives of John, Sharon, Lisa, Sandra, and others will give you the hope and courage to forgive.

Summary of Chapter One

1. There are four parts to complete forgiveness: experiencing God's forgiveness, giving forgiveness to those who have wronged us, seeking forgiveness from those we have wronged, and rebuilding broken relationships.
2. Experiencing God's forgiveness requires that we accept Jesus Christ as our Savior, and then function in the truth of His love for us as His children.
3. Giving forgiveness means that I no longer hold anyone responsible for the things they do or say to wrong me.
4. Seeking forgiveness means I humble myself, admitting my wrong to the person wronged, and asking to be released from the responsibility of "paying for" that sin.
5. God desires rebuilt relationships. We are told to reconcile with our brothers and sisters in Christ. All that is required is the willingness to allow Christ to love that person through you.
6. It is pride or fear that keeps me from experiencing every phase of forgiveness.

The Freedom to Love and Live Again

Chapter Two

My Childhood Could Not Have Been Worse

(Story told by John)

The best way to begin this story is to go back quite a few years. I warn you that some of the details of this story may seem gross or sick. Perhaps the level of depravity in my story will help you to understand the magnitude of the healing that can come through true forgiveness.

My father's father was gassed during World War I. He spent his life slowly dying of leukemia. He was an alcoholic who worked his way through five wives. Two of the wives lived in insane asylums, including the woman who became my father's mother. She originally had entered the asylum when she was about 7 years old, and spent the rest of her life going in and out of the asylum, eventually dying there at the age of 83.

My grandfather was too drunk to care for his children, so when my grandmother went into the asylum the state took over their children. The children lived in many different orphanages. My father would often escape and try to help his siblings break out, too. He tried to provide for them by stealing, hustling, or eating out of trash cans. Whatever it took.

Somehow the children always ended up back home with my grandfather. Social workers would catch them and put them back in the orphanages. They spent a lot of time on the run. My father told me that when the children were sent back to the orphanage, the workers would beat them intensely, to discourage them from escaping again. My uncle had permanent scars on his back from the beatings. I never saw scars on the outside of my father, but they were definitely there on the inside.

The Freedom to Love and Live Again

Some of the sisters and the priest at a church orphanage sexually molested my father and his sister. So he grew up very bitter, angry, and resentful towards the church.

At 16 my father talked his father into signing him over to military service. My father enlisted in the Navy, went overseas, and joined the fighting during World War II. He was blown out of a couple of ships but survived, eventually transferring into a more specialized force.

At one point during the war, he and a friend were walking together down a road. Without warning, his friend's head was blown off right before my father's eyes. My father went berserk and started firing bullets into the heads of dead enemy bodies lying on the ground. He was medically discharged for this breach of military etiquette.

After the discharge he spent a year in the hospital, trying to get his head straight. When he got out of the hospital, he was married and had two children with whom I have never had contact.

Then my grandfather died, sending my father all the way over the edge. His relationship with his wife eroded to the point that he tried to throw her out a window. A short time later he committed assault with a deadly weapon, shooting a car full of bullets with a machine gun.

He was convicted of attempted murder and spent five years in prison. His wife divorced him. After serving the full five years, he got out and met my mother. He was 30 and my mom was only 17.

My mother also had a difficult childhood. Her mother and father didn't want her. Her mother had some mental problems, so they gave her up to grandparents who raised her for a long time. Then she lived with an aunt for a while.

When my father got out of jail he became a pimp and had quite a few prostitutes working for him. Later, my mom and dad were married and had three children: myself, followed by twins, my younger brother and sister. I remember a time when three prostitutes were actually baby-sitting for us in our house.

Another early memory is of my father bringing home a safe with a group of his buddies. He was a thief on the side, and they were trying to crack the safe open. The situation was, needless to say, unusual.

Between the pimping and the thieving my father ended up working for the FBI, probably as an informant to keep himself out of jail. The FBI relocated us to Mexico for a year, then we moved on to Arizona, where we've lived ever since.

This was when I began to realize that things weren't exactly normal in my family. The first time I can remember my father trying to sodomize me, I was five years old. It was horrible and very painful, so he eventually stopped. However, he encouraged me to sodomize my brother and sister who were each about three years old.

I remember him helping me get an erection and then helping me insert it. He encouraged me to have sex with my sister because he liked to watch and listen. Finally, my father began ordering me to perform oral sex on him. This went on until I was thirteen.

I learned a lot about prayer.

In addition to the sex acts with my siblings and the oral sex on my father, we were also subjected to three forms of punishment: pain, humiliation, or separation.

The pain was administered by my father with a garden hose. My typical punishment was 10 whacks with the garden hose if I was disobedient. A garden hose leaves a pretty good-sized welt, so my mother often doctored me, putting salve on my back until I healed. I frequently stayed home from school to let my wounds heal.

Humiliation was the second method of punishment. My father was a master of humiliation. When I was five I had a problem controlling bowel movements. It is possible that the sodomy started when I was younger than five and actually caused my lack of control. When I had an accident, my father would take my underwear and smear the excrement in my underwear on my face. Then he would put the underwear on my head and stand me in the corner and let the feces dry on my face.

In one particular instance my father had a visitor when I was standing in the corner. I remember the man commenting about it and my father saying, "Well, this is just his punishment for not controlling his bowel movements."

The third form of discipline was separation from family and activities. This took the form of kneeling or standing in a corner. There were times where I knelt in the corner from 8:00 at night until 4:00 in the morning, when my mother would finally come to get me. I couldn't even walk from kneeling so long. My mom lifted me up and carried me to the bedroom to put me to sleep.

Needless to say there was much physical and verbal abuse in my life. My brother and sister and I became experts at avoiding my father as he walked from one room to the next. We tried to time his steps. As he walked into a room we walked out of it. We prayed every day that he wouldn't catch us. It didn't take much to upset him, and we never knew what might spark him. It was sheer torment.

At the age of 12, I came to know the Lord through a friend in school. Since kindergarten, this friend had been a very prominent figure in my life. He was very gifted and excelled at everything he did. Not only did he know the Lord, but his parents were also very active Christians. He was really into the Word at a very young age and was an inspiration to me. For a long time, I admired him from a distance. But somehow, somewhere our paths crossed and he befriended me and led me to the Lord. We went to church together. We even started our own neighborhood Bible study.

Through this experience I began to realize there was something terribly wrong with my life. I had always thought everyone's life was filled with the same abuse as mine. I had been praying for a long time, so I had a sense of God's presence even in the turmoil. But I was very confused and in pain about why I was being subjected to these torments.

"Why Lord," I would pray, "must I do this to my father? Why must I have sex with my sister?" I knew something was wrong. I was hurting and I couldn't figure out why the Lord was doing this or allowing it to happen to me. I thought it must be because everybody else was doing the same thing. I couldn't talk to anyone about it. My father encouraged us not to say a word to anybody.

I was sure the neighbors sensed that something was wrong, but no one ever said or did anything. They also seemed to be afraid of my father. I could see fear in their eyes when he talked to them. I didn't know what to do and I was very confused and angry.

When I came to know the Lord, however, I began to feel like I had a life. My friend was leading me to new experiences and encouraging me to be strong, even though he didn't know what I was going through at home. I never told him. But I felt protected by his sense of strength whenever I was with him.

Because of the abuse at home, I was a walking target in school. I got a concussion every year, usually from being hit in the head by other kids, or from some other serious accident. I was always being beat up on or picked on. In seventh grade, even the girls ganged up on me, picking me up and throwing me into a bathroom. They destroyed my clothes and did things to humiliate me. I couldn't get away from the abuse. The world seemed to be just as bad as home. There was no peace or rest anywhere.

My Christian friend and my Christian experience gave me some strength and a bit of peace. When I was 13 I was invited to a camp-out with his church. I planned to go. Two days before that camp-out my father asked me to perform oral sex on him. I refused and he said I couldn't go on the camp-out.

This was the first time I said "no" to my father's demands for pleasure. He became very angry, saying, "You stay in your room until you give in or you won't go on the camp-out." I stayed in my room and prayed, "Lord, I sure do want to go on this camp-out and I sure don't want to do this sex act on my father any more. I've had it."

On the morning of the camp-out I didn't know whether I was going or not, but I had my bags packed, hoping the Lord would deliver. My father let me go. That was the beginning of my independence.

But as my father began to lose control over me he became angrier and more violent. He still wanted me to have sex with my sister so that he could listen. He encouraged me to seek her out in the middle of the night. Or he would tell my sister to come to me. It was not a good situation.

And situations outside my home reinforced my embarrassment about sex. Once a girl from my neighborhood encouraged me to take my clothes off. I was very embarrassed and felt horrible about it. I was very uncomfortable being naked in front of this girl and did not find any pleasure in it. Because I was so embarrassed I went and confessed it to my mother and father. My father would soon use this information to cover-up his crimes.

The Freedom to Love and Live Again

When I was thirteen I suffered another trauma at my father's hands. He decided that I was not able to climax sexually, or that I didn't know how. So he used this as an excuse to force me to have sex with my mother. He set my mother up to come in while I was in the shower and he made me have sex with her. I know this was very painful for her. She apologized but said that she was trying to do what Dad wanted her to do.

(My mother, unbeknownst to me, began having nervous break-downs shortly after she married my father. When I was nineteen, a series of breakdowns put her in the hospital. She was medicated into a non-functional, almost vegetative state. When she came home she was incapable of cooking dinner or cleaning the house. Basically, she just sat.

My father seemed to be duplicating a generational pattern of putting wives into mental institutions. At that time I didn't know anything about mental illness in general, or her mental illness in particular, but I could see how much she depended on my father. She was willing to do almost anything he said because she was very afraid of him.)

After Mom and I had sex a few times, I felt a burning sensation when I urinated and had to go to the hospital. I was getting ready to go into the doctor's office when my father told me to tell the doctor that I had had sex with the girl from my neighborhood. I did not want to lie to the doctor. I hadn't had sex with the girl; I only took my clothes off in front of her. I was very upset that my father would encourage me to tell this lie. I didn't realize that he was actually protecting what had gone on between my mother and me until years later.

Part of the surgical procedure they performed on me was to put a catheter into me while I was awake. They told me that the catheter had little razor blades and that they were cleaning out the garbage that was causing the burning in my urinary tract. To this day, I don't really know the truth about all that. I suspect that I had caught a venereal disease from my Mom.

A short time later my father came down with Valley fever, a lung disease caused by breathing the fine dust in Arizona, and was instructed by the doctor to move. They pulled me out of high school after only six months. I had just begun a new phase in my life, in which my new friend was helping me to grow in the Lord. This separation crushed me.

I became very angry with God and thought that He was ripping my new life from me. I was very upset and asked my friend when he would come to visit me. He encouraged me, saying that the Lord probably wanted me to be independent from him and be a leader on my own. I didn't know what independence or leadership looked like. They were completely foreign concepts to me. All I knew was that I was very angry.

Without my friend, I was thrown back into the situation with my father. I had nowhere to run. My new school was in the northern part of the state. I was in a strange new area and I was very timid and weak. I was abused horribly, from being beaten by gangs, having my hair cut off with knives, to simply being tormented day after day.

Now my father, for some unknown reason, insisted that I be baptized Mormon. That was completely against my Christian beliefs and I didn't want to do it. But, in submission to him, I got baptized, pushing things further over the edge for me.

The physical violence from my father became more frequent. He stopped using the rubber hose on me and just hit me with his hands whenever he was angry. My mother and father fought more and more. My father drank steadily, combining the alcohol with steroid use. He came down with Valley fever again, and then with malaria he had first caught while in the service.

He suffered through fevers and chills regularly. He became a lunatic and would fly off the handle at any time for any reason.

Finally, when I was eighteen, my father and I got into a fight. His violence became too much for me and I rebelled. I left home to find a new independence. I had never experienced the world apart from my family because they were very, very controlling people. The world outside was a whole new experience for me.

* * *

What a horrible story John has to tell. His experiences as a child are as horrific and awful as any we can imagine. We all have heard how childhood abuse can haunt people for the rest of their lives, interfering with everything that they try to do.

How will John react? Will his life become a wasteland, devoid of love and hope? or will he rise above his pain to live and love again?

Surprisingly, the answer is, <u>both</u>.

Chapter Three

Why Forgive?

By human standards, John has every "right" not to forgive his father. Why would he? Why forgive a father for maliciously abusing his son? Why forgive a man who uses his son as a sex toy? What motivation does John have to give forgiveness?

Why forgive a drunk driver who broadsides you after running a stop sign? Why forgive the bully at school who picks on you and calls you names? Why forgive a wife or a husband who walks out of a marriage? Why forgive that person who gives you a nasty look on the freeway? Why forgive the boss who is always criticizing you?

We live in a world full of abuse. The need to give forgiveness is ever present. As long as we reside on this planet, there will be reason to give forgiveness. But what is the benefit? Why forgive?

Scripture is full of reasons to forgive. If we need motivation, we need only to search the Word of God. John and others have discovered that there are many valid reasons to give forgiveness rather than harbor grudges.

The greatest motivation to forgive others is that Christ Jesus forgave us and made us righteous. *And when you were dead in your transgressions and the uncircumcision of your flesh, He made you alive together with Him, having forgiven us all our transgressions* (Colossians 2:13). *He made Him who knew no sin to be sin on our behalf, that we might become the righteousness of God in Him* (2 Corinthians 5:21).

Wow! What more motivation do we need? In the depth of our depravity, the Almighty God of the universe sent His perfectly sinless Son, Jesus Christ, to <u>become sin</u>, so that we might become the righteousness of God. If we are the righteousness of God, what keeps us from forgiving others when they wrong us?

Ephesians 4:32 says, *And be kind to one another, tender-hearted, forgiving each other, just as God in Christ also has forgiven you.*

The words "forgiving" and "forgiven" come from the same Greek root word as "grace". Grace means "a favor done without expectation of return; lovingkindness that finds its only motive in the bounty and free-heartedness of the giver; unearned and unmerited favor."

How much favor have you earned? NONE! How much has Christ "graced" you? TOTALLY! How much favor have the persons earned who have wronged you? NONE! How much should you "grace" them? TOTALLY!

For John to do the impossible, forgive his father, he must realize the significance of what Christ did for him. He must realize how deep his own need of forgiveness is. That is motivation for him to forgive, just as God in Christ has forgiven him.

Have you realized the greatness of your need for the Savior's complete forgiveness? Do you realize that He offers you complete forgiveness now? It is a free gift that must be accepted so that you, too, can forgive others as Christ has forgiven you. Forgiveness depends not on what we do, but on what Christ has already done.

The second motivation, that John found in scripture, to give forgiveness is the choice to break a generational pattern of habit. *...yet He will by no means leave the guilty unpunished, visiting the iniquity of fathers on the children and on the grandchildren to the third and fourth generations* (Exodus 34:7b). John's grandfather was abusive to John's father, who was abusive to John. A pattern was established. The iniquity (sin) of fathers was visiting children and grandchildren. At least three generations of physical abusiveness set John up to abuse his wife and kids as well.

Not all sin is generational; we come up with much of it on our own. However, if there is a history of substance abuse, lying, divorce, physical abuse, manipulation, adultery, or other sin in your family, you are prone to perpetuate the pattern of sin.

The real truth is, John has a choice whether or not to allow the pattern to continue, and so do you. You have no excuse to act the way previous generations acted. By the grace of God, you are free to choose righteousness!

The laws of sowing and reaping illustrate the third motivation to give forgiveness. God commands it and we have a choice to obey or disobey. Every choice, right or wrong, has consequences.

Just as a farmer sows seed in the springtime and reaps a harvest in the fall, we make choices that will have effects on our lives.

There are four laws of sowing and reaping:

1. You reap what you sow.
2. You reap more than you sow.
3. You reap in proportion to what you sow.
4. You reap in a later season.

Let me illustrate:

YOU REAP WHAT YOU SOW

If a farmer plants seeds of wheat, what will grow? Wheat, of course. John's grandfather and father sowed seeds of unrighteousness. What was harvested? Corruption. Is it surprising that God has something to say about that? Look at Galatians 6:7-8: *Do not be deceived, God is not mocked; for whatever a man sows, this he will also reap. For the one who sows to his own flesh shall from the flesh reap corruption, but the one who sows to the Spirit shall from the Spirit reap eternal life.* God will not be made a fool of. Your sin (unforgiveness) will find you out (Numbers 32:23). His laws are more certain than the laws of gravity or thermodynamics!

YOU REAP MORE THAN YOU SOW

For they sow the wind, and they reap the whirlwind (Hosea 8:7a). The farmer who plants one kernel of corn will not reap only one newly grown kernel, will he? He will reap an entire plant, with many ears. So it is with whatever we sow. Have you ever told one little lie, then had to tell a bigger, riskier one to cover up the first? Didn't the lies get out of hand after a while? That is because we reap more than we sow. When John's grandfather took his first drink of alcohol, was he planning to become violent later in life? Was he planning for that drink to have great consequence in later generations? I doubt it. But it did. Such is the case with our own sin.

Have you sown "small seeds" of corruption? Perhaps you have held a grudge against someone. It isn't a big grudge, and you don't intend for it to be harmful down the road. Maybe you are just a little "ticked-off." That is a seed that is sown. A harvest will come. That is motivation to forgive.

YOU REAP IN PROPORTION TO WHAT YOU SOW

The Lord of the harvest says, *he who sows sparingly shall also reap sparingly; and he who sows bountifully shall also reap bountifully* (2 Corinthians 9:6). John's father and grandfather sowed corruption often. Proportionately, their reaping of corruption was almost constant. Their families were filled with turmoil from sunrise to sunset.

Likewise, John was faced with a choice. Would he sow seeds of hatred and bitterness sparingly, bountifully, or not at all? You will find out in the very next chapter.

But before we hear the end of his story, let's hear <u>your</u> story. Are you sowing the seeds of love and forgiveness bountifully? If so, you are probably reaping a harvest of joy, peace, and contentment. If, however, you are sowing seeds of anger, bitterness, or resentment, even sparingly, you can expect a rotten harvest.

YOU REAP IN A LATER SEASON

The Word of God encourages us to be diligent in doing good: *And let us not lose heart in doing good, for in due time we shall reap if we do not grow weary* (Galatians 6:9). To choose to be diligent in John's case requires a dependence upon the Lord to love his father through him. John made that choice, as you will see in Chapter Four. He was motivated to give forgiveness to his father because he anticipated a harvest of love and life.

Are you experiencing a difficult relationship with a person who is impossible to love? Be diligent to sow seeds of forgiveness. God's promise is that you will reap a wonderful harvest of love.

Another motivation John had for giving forgiveness to his father and grandfather was that, if he did <u>not</u> forgive them, the effects of their abuse would carry over to his wife, his kids, and others that he loves. There are many ramifications when a person chooses to live in unforgiveness. If that person has a grudge against someone, it may trigger an emotion that results in an angry reaction such as: "You remind me so much of your mother when you do that." The offended person may then begin to treat the "offender" as they would treat the mother if she were there, even though the "offender" may be totally unaware of the cause. Innocent people often get hurt this way.

Why Forgive?

In your life, is there someone who really has not offended you in any way, but reminds you of someone who <u>has</u> offended you? Until now, you may not have realized what that little tension between the two of you was rooted in. If that is the case, you have additional motivation to give forgiveness to that person who has wronged you, so the relationship with the person who reminds you of the offender can grow in love.

There are at least two other motivations to forgive those who offend us. One is so that you move out of the way, and give the Lord "room" to do His purifying work in the life of the offender. When you fail to forgive someone, you are actually taking some degree of vengeance. Though there may be no outward signs of vengeance, you secretly want them to "get what's coming to them." So, you hold them guilty until they "get it."

Romans 12:19 says, *Never take your own revenge, beloved, but leave room for the wrath of God, for it is written, "Vengeance is Mine, I will repay," says the Lord.* God is sovereign, as we will discuss in Chapter Seven, and knows the very best way to deal with each of us. If you are effecting vengeance on the offender, you are playing god.

When John chose to forgive his dad, imagine how that opened the door for the Lord to deal with John's father. Do you suppose it brought conviction? Do you suppose it had an affect on the relationship between John and his father?

God, the Father, is watching over and intending to care for every one of His precious children. He, and He alone, has the power to do what needs to be done in every person's life to bring them freedom. Without His power it would be impossible for us to forgive others.

And finally, perhaps the most exciting motivation for giving forgiveness is that forgiveness is a doorway between freedom and bondage, between life and death, between blessings and curses. *"I call heaven and earth to witness against you today, that I have set before you life and death, the blessing and the curse. So choose life in order that you may live, you and your descendants"* (Deuteronomy 30:19). We are commanded to forgive. Obedience results in freedom, life and blessings. Jesus said, *"I came that they might have life, and might have it abundantly"* (John 10:10b). Our

Lord <u>wants</u> us to experience life abundantly. He <u>wants</u> us to experience blessing and freedom. And He makes it possible.

As you will read, John, Lisa, Sandra, and others chose freedom, life and blessings. They realized Christ's abundant love and forgiveness of them and they aimed that love and forgiveness at those who wronged them. They are at peace with God and with the offenders. They experience the overwhelming joy of the incredible life of the Lord Jesus.

Perhaps you have chosen bondage, death, and curses. Maybe you are being eaten up from the inside out. The prison of unforgiveness has you penned behind bars of anger, resentment, bitterness, and malice. If so, you hold the keys and those keys will be explained in Chapter Eight. But all you must do to escape from Satan's torment is to insert the keys you hold. You cannot fully experience God's love if you are imprisoned, being tormented by the enemy.

The bitterness may be causing you not to enjoy other relationships as well. Bitter people are not fun to be around. People in bondage often try to bring others into bondage with them. They will treat others poorly out of the emotions of resentment and anger. Why not be free? Why not forgive?

* * *

John's grandfather and father certainly sowed the seeds for John to grow up to be just like them. The damage was done. John's life is wrecked and he's about to pass on a ruined life to his children ... the fourth generation. What good is forgiveness at this point? It's too late for forgiveness. After all, John's father should seek John's forgiveness. John is the victim, isn't he?

These are defeating thoughts that will destroy a person's life. Yes, damage is done, but all is not lost. John's life is not wrecked, and neither is yours. The generational sins do not have to continue. It is never too late for forgiveness, and if you wait for someone to ask you to forgive them, you may never get the opportunity.

Our gracious Lord gives us plenty of motivation to give forgiveness to those that have wronged or offended us. How will you respond to the motivation?

Read how John responded.

Summary of Chapter Three

1. There are at least six motivations to give forgiveness:
   - Because Jesus Christ has forgiven us.
   - To break the pattern of generational sin.
   - Because of the laws of sowing and reaping.
   - Because the bitterness, anger, and resentment may carry over to those we love.
   - To see God carry out His plan for our lives and the lives of those who have hurt us.
   - To enjoy freedom, life, and blessings rather than bondage, death, and curses.
2. It is never too late to forgive.
3. It is never useless to forgive.

The Freedom to Love and Live Again

Chapter Four

Forgiving the Unforgivable

(Story told by John)

After leaving home, where I had been controlled completely for eighteen years, I went wild. I drank and took drugs. I had an identity problem because of my sexual past. My father had accused me of being gay because I would not have sex with anybody outside the family. I didn't have a girlfriend.

I admit that I was intimidated by girls and afraid of them. But I also had moral convictions, due to my faith, and still considered myself a virgin. Even though I knew about sex, from my father's "orientation course", I didn't know if what I had learned was right or wrong. I was really confused.

I decided to start experimenting sexually with other women. The relationships were tumultuous. The excitement just wasn't there for me, so I needed to have different women all the time. Some would complain that I would reject them after sex. I had no clue. I didn't sense that I was rejecting them, but I became very cold and distant after sex.

I went through many years of being a rebel, doing drugs and drinking, trying to kill the pain. However, I did manage to maintain one relationship for four years. When it ended, I fell apart. My whole identity had been wrapped up in that relationship. It seemed that this woman was the only person who had ever really loved me and accepted me as I was. She knew all about my abuse and seemed to understand me and accept me. When she called it off I was crushed and devastated.

I was twenty-three years old and contemplating suicide. Everything was crashing down around me. I ceased to function. Then I saw a program on television about depression. I talked to my dad and said, "I think I have a problem. I think its called depression." He took me to my mother's doctor and I began counseling.

The Freedom to Love and Live Again

Before my first day of counseling, my mother and father were in great turmoil. My mother was angry, fearing that I would open up family secrets and talk to someone about what had happened. She was afraid my father was going to be thrown in jail and she insisted that I should not tell what had happened. I tried to assure her that her fears would not come true. I believed that the therapist would be required to keep my story confidential. And, of course, he did.

My first therapy session must have lasted two hours. I remember coming home emotionally upset. I was living next door to my parents at the time. When I went to their house, my mom was doing the laundry. My dad started one of his famous fights that didn't have any logic. He cornered me and insisted, all of a sudden, that we fight. It came to blows. I had never thrown blows at my father before, only put my hands up in defense. I was still convicted that I should never hit my father. He said, "Oh, you're going to fight me!" I said, "No. But I'm not going to let you hurt me any more." He went ballistic.

My mother called the police and the police pulled him off me. He was trying to choke me to death as he pinned me to the washer and dryer. The police made me leave the house and directed me to stay away from my father while I continued therapy.

I was in and out of group and solo therapy sessions for the next few years, mostly for my depression, but they never really seemed to solve any of my problems. I knew there was something missing in my life, but I didn't know how to find it. The solution, I decided, was love. But how do you find love in this day and age?

I did it the old-fashioned way. I got married.

I was twenty-nine years old and thought, "This is it!" I believed that marrying Rachel would teach me about love, and love would solve my problems. Although I wasn't walking after the Lord, I still believed there was only one way that our marriage would work, and that was by having God be part of it. I felt very convicted about that.

I told Rachel, "I don't know much about marriage, I don't know much about being a father, and I don't know much about being a husband because I never really learned those things. But I think I do know one thing. If our marriage is going to survive, it is only going to survive with God participating in the relationship."

Those were beautiful words, but I was still a rebel. Though I knew God was the answer, I was unwilling to submit to God on any issue. Within a week of our wedding all hell broke loose!

We very quickly realized that we were in trouble. Not only did we not get along; we were almost ready to kill each other. I'm still amazed that we held on and didn't get a divorce right then.

The source of our conflict was a classic battle for control of the marriage. I had been controlled all my life and I was not going to be controlled again. This was no minor skirmish. My wife attempted suicide a couple of times. She did not want me to go to work because of her insecurity. I would go anyway, which escalated the situation. Rachel ended up spending some time in a very prominent hospital in California that dealt with mental illness.

Here I was, repeating the cycle of my father and grandfather, putting my wife into a mental hospital. Rachel came out of the hospital two weeks later, but she was very unstable. We were fighting again almost immediately, and I ended up calling the police.

Rachel stood at the door, blocking my path with a butcher's knife. She wouldn't let me leave. My counter-attack consisted of trying to wrap the telephone cord around her neck, and threatening to kill her if she didn't stop what she was doing.

Our marriage and our lives were deteriorating very rapidly. Once again, we sought counseling.

Our first counseling experience was very unique. The counselor charged us ninety dollars to tell us that we probably shouldn't be married. I wanted to reach across the desk, grab the counselor by the throat, and ask for my money back! I wanted to say, "Thank you very much for charging me ninety dollars to tell us something I already knew."

Rachel and I were very dependent on each other, even though we wanted to kill each other, so we stayed together. We went to counselor after counselor after counselor but never really got the help we needed. We knew that God was still missing from our lives, so we decided to go to church more. My wife was brought up Catholic, so we went to her church.

That didn't help, but in the process, we were guided to a couple of Christian counseling agencies. They tried to help, but seemed to focus on secular psychological counseling rather than finding answers through God. They charged on a sliding scale, but we were still running out of money fast.

We needed to be counseled two or three times a week sometimes. We needed a personal baby-sitter most of the time just to keep us from killing each other.

Given my childhood, it's not surprising that we also had sexual problems. Rachel felt rejected. My sex drive completely ended after we got married. I thought, "Boy, now I'm married and I'm comfortable. I don't have to do this sex thing any more." Rachel was in shock, feeling totally rejected, and not understanding why.

I had no sex drive and didn't want to have anything to do with her. Yet, somehow, we did manage to conceive children, which just intensified the tension in our household.

The police visited a couple more times, investigating reports of domestic violence, and we became desperate to solve our problems. We finally found a church that we felt comfortable with, and my wife came to know the Lord.

Through friends and our new church we began to have fellowship with other believers. The Lord, through that fellowship, led us to Victorious Christian Living, International (VCL), a biblical discipleship counseling and training center.

Through the teachings and counseling we received at VCL, the Lord worked his ministry of forgiveness and reconciliation in my wife and me. Everything the counselors said made perfect sense. We wanted to argue or disagree, but we couldn't.

The truths we received from the Word were cutting, like a two-edged sword. They hit us right between the eyes. We continued to struggle and fall, but for the first time we began to know and understand the truth. We began to know how to correct our situation.

Through this ministry of reconciliation and forgiveness we began repairing the broken pieces of our lives. We saw how we had been reacting to one another, using our hurt and rejection to try and change the other's behavior. We learned that the victim is guilty for taking fleshly methods to protect or react to what others do to us. When we no longer acted out of our flesh, our relationship as husband and wife immediately began to improve.

We discovered that we became new people in Christ and finally understood exactly what that meant. We also discovered that God had given us the power of His life by the Holy Spirit to forgive as Christ forgave. This made it possible for us to forgive one another for all the hurts we had caused.

Moreover, the supernatural power of Christ's forgiveness made it possible for me to do the impossible: forgive my father! That forgiveness included no longer holding a grudge against him for what he had done to me, no longer having negative feelings, no longer holding him guilty.

Wow! That's huge!

Through our relationship with the Lord and understanding <u>how</u> to forgive, Rachel and I were both able to go back and reconcile with my father. My father and I now have a forgiving and loving relationship after all these years. My mother has been taken off her medication and we're seeing the Lord work in her life, too.

Rachel and I are now able to be a witness and a testimony to my mother and father. To see these changes work so quickly and so dramatically, to have a loving relationship with my father, after all these years, is only possible through the dynamic life of Christ Jesus.

Because I was able to forgive, I experience my father pulling me aside to tell me how much he loves me. The feeling this gives me is truly incredible.

By following our example, my father now gives hugs readily. He tells me how nice it is to see how my children are being raised. He is amazed how I love them, spend time with them, and discipline them when they need it.

After all the pain and suffering we now see the Lord raising up a new generation, our children, as well as my wife and me. The generational cycle of destruction has been broken.

The physical and emotional pain caused by my father's daily rituals of sex and violence has been healed. Christ's ministry of forgiveness and reconciliation has literally raised the dead, if you consider my family's past. To have my father see and recognize the new life that is being birthed in my children, in my life with the Lord, and my wife's life is nothing short of a miracle.

The only way I can conclude my story is to say that I am reminded of Christ dying on the cross and suffering so much at the hands of us as human beings. Christ, being absolutely sinless and born into this world having done nothing wrong, was still tortured and put to death on the cross. And through all His pain and agony, He asked His father, God, to forgive us for what we were doing to Him.

So who am I not to forgive my father, and not seek his forgiveness? Christ did that much for me. That is the least I can do for my father after what has been done for me by Jesus.

I praise the Lord that He is great and can restore life. He can still raise people from the dead. There is a Kingdom life to be lived here on earth, which I didn't think was possible. I believe the Lord is now using me in the ministry of reconciliation and calling me to full time pastoral ministry in accordance to 2 Corinthians 5:17, **Therefore, if any man is in Christ, he is a new creature; the old things passed away; behold, new things have come.**

"Thanks, Dave, for letting me tell this story of the freedom and love that come as a result of forgiveness."

* * *

As you read the conclusion to John's tale, how did you feel? Were you imagining yourself in his shoes? Were you wondering if, given the same circumstances, you would have been able to forgive, as he has done?

Perhaps John is a unique person, one whom we cannot hope to emulate. Maybe his supernatural power to forgive is beyond our limited grasp.

Not so! John simply learned, and then <u>embraced</u>, three universal truths that allowed him to tap into Christ's supernatural power of forgiveness. And now <u>you</u> can learn them too!

Chapter Five

Godship: The Root of All Offenses

(Story told by LuAnn)

John learned some pretty significant things that enabled him to forgive his father and grandfather, and to experience the freedom to love and live again. He took some specific steps in giving forgiveness, which we will share in Chapter Eight. However, there were other scriptural truths he embraced before he actually gave forgiveness. Let's look at some of those truths as we prepare to forgive.

The first truth John embraced was that God is God and he is not! It is always dangerous to try to "play god," since we don't have the power to do so. I will illustrate with LuAnn's story:

As I began to write, I thought I would be telling a simple story, about adultery and forgiveness. But this story has become much more than that. It is a testimony to the faithful Father who, with a gentle hand, is conforming one of His children into the likeness of His First-Born. This conforming work is a process.

Before I married, I believed that meaning came from other people approving and accepting me. From this worldly point of view, I thought that I needed to work to achieve others' standards of value. To me those standards were: be fun, be successful, and be attractive. To feel valued in accordance with these standards I wanted men to find me attractive and pursue me. As a result of this belief system I went into debt having fun and spending money to look good. I compromised my health through bulimia and several immoral relationships.

I reached a spiritual low as my pursuit of the world emptied me of joy, peace, and love. Then the Lord began to draw me back to Himself. That's when I met Rocky. During the three years we dated, my relationship with the Lord was slowly restored. But I still did not trust that He was "Enough God." This lack of trust continued to manifest itself in my pursuit of other people's acceptance. I was still bulimic and vulnerable to a man finding me attractive and pursuing me.

When Rocky asked me to marry him, I was convicted that it was the Lord's will for me. I was faced with a decision to live in obedience to God and find my acceptance in Him. That would include being faithful to my husband, not choosing to stay single, and not letting the number of men that love me be the measure of my value. The pursuit of worldly things had brought only living death: emptiness, torment, insecurity, inadequacy, and inferiority. I knew that Jesus alone had the words of life. As I married Rocky, I said, "Yes, Lord," and began to walk in obedience.

In spite of many areas of victory, one part of my life was tragically out of line with God's plan and will. My relationship with my husband was affectionate, fun, and a source of great happiness. But our union was shallow. There was a void I sensed but could not see.

I began to pray Ephesians 1:17-20 for my husband and myself. **...that the God of our Lord Jesus Christ, the Father of glory, may give to you a spirit of wisdom and of revelation in the knowledge of Him. I pray that the eyes of your heart may be enlightened, so that you may know what is the hope of His calling, what are the riches of the glory of His inheritance in the saints, and what is the surpassing greatness of His power toward us who believe. These are in accordance with the working of the strength of His might which He brought about in Christ, when He raised Him from the dead, and seated Him at His right hand in the heavenly places.**

Three years later, in Life Ministry Training (LMT) at VCL International, the sense of something lacking in our marriage had grown into frustration and anger, and a definite need to forgive. During the LMT ministry time I expressed these feelings about my marriage to my ministry partner. She listened, asked questions and then made the following observation. "I see two people together, in this marriage, but very much alone."

I was hearing the truth, but it conflicted with what I wanted to believe. I had always believed that "a marriage between two affectionate people who 'never fight' should be a good marriage."

The Lord began to convict me that in every area of weakness and need in my life, I confided in friends, spiritual leaders, siblings and parents but never shared myself with my husband. I had carefully constructed a wall around the real me and had covered it with signs that said, "All is well. I'm strong. Don't worry about me. Do not enter. If you don't understand all that, let me put it more clearly: Keep out!"

If a marriage partner thinks they must hide emotions from their spouse, something is wrong in the relationship. I disclosed nothing. I had strategically avoided vulnerability throughout my life. I protected myself from the person I loved the most. I feared him seeing my sinfulness, my imperfections, my weaknesses, and my needs. I believed that if he knew me, he might not love me.

I had prayed that God would "open the eyes of my understanding." The Lord was answering my prayer. He was giving me a "revelation in the knowledge of Jesus Christ," His knowledge of me. I was beginning to see myself and our marriage through His eyes. I realized that I was trying to be the god of my life and of our marriage. The sin that plagued my life was "godship."

"Godship" is allowing any circumstance or person, including myself, to rule my life instead of God, my Lord, and the Creator of the universe.

It was LuAnn's godship (sin) that created a need for repentance and giving forgiveness. She did not relate properly to her husband. Instead, she set standards and demanded that they be met. For example, Rocky was expected to love her a certain way, without having to be told, or LuAnn would resent him. Why was there a need to forgive? Because LuAnn set the standard, demanded obedience to the standard, and judged Rocky if he didn't meet the standard. Resentment toward another person stems from the thought, "That person should not treat me that way." She was allowing circumstances and feelings to control her.

Godship is the root of all offenses, and is exhibited in many different ways. When you function without taking into account what God has to say, you are functioning in godship. When you live by the world's standards rather than God's, you are living in godship. When you allow circumstances or feelings to control you, you are playing god. When you walk after the flesh, doing whatever you please, you are walking in godship.

That creates a need to give forgiveness because you hold someone else responsible. Even John exercised godship in relating to his father. He reacted wrongly to things that were said and done to him. But John learned, as LuAnn did, to take responsibility for his actions and attitudes, regardless of how others treated them.

* * *

LuAnn was getting the picture: if we play god, it will always backfire, resulting in the need to experience the Lord's love and forgiveness, give forgiveness, seek forgiveness, and rebuild broken relationships. Her relationship with Rocky was in need of those things.

The Lord was also moving in my husband's life. His hunger for the Lord grew, as I had never seen in our relationship before. He began to say that he was 'seeing' his life as he had never seen it before. He expressed that in his pursuit of wealth he had become spiritually bankrupt and it disgusted him. He decided to shut down his business and move our family. He no longer desired the riches of the world. Now his desire was to become rich in the things of God. As he heard the testimonies of people who had completed the counseling and/or discipleship training at VCL International, he longed to know the power of God in his life that he saw in theirs. He was jealous of their knowledge of and life with the Lord.

Rocky shut down the business and we moved to Phoenix to begin the third level of VCLI courses, Training in Discipleship (TID). During the time between LMT and TID training, I did not share my heart or the events of my life with my husband as the Lord had impressed me to do. When TID began, the Lord wasted no time in using my trainer to articulate the steps of obedience he was calling me to.

My Holy Spirit "homework" was still self-disclosure.

I took the first step in being transparent with my husband by telling him the deep dark secret that had begun my life of self-protection. I told Rocky that when I was 12 I had been sexually molested. When I took that step of obedience light began to flood our marriage. Rocky saw me for the first time as he had never seen me before. To him, it was as if the fog around me had begun to clear.

Two months later, at dinner one night, Rocky took my hands as his eyes filled with tears and said, "Lu, I've been unfaithful." It felt as if a knife had plunged to a depth I didn't know I possessed. I was in a state of shock and could hardly comprehend what I had been told. I felt as if I was on a turbulent sea tossing to and fro. My stomach shut down and seemed to send a message to my head, "Closed indefinitely." I was facing a reality that I had never imagined but yet somehow always knew. For I knew I had not had my husband. My husband's first love had been his company and I knew another woman shared that work with him. She had been his helpmate in the things that mattered most to him.

* * *

This is a definite case of "double godship!" Rocky, we discover, had allowed circumstances (pursuing the riches of this world) and feelings (becoming intimately interested in another woman) to control his life. In the process, everyone got hurt. Playing god always leads to a need for forgiveness.

But notice what happened before ANY forgiveness took place: Rocky and LuAnn each realized the godship in their own lives! Each began to take responsibility for their own actions, apart from how the other was treating them. Often, forgiveness "doesn't work" because the standards are never dropped. Thus, responsibility is never taken.

Only when we admit, "I am responsible for my reactions toward the people who hurt me," and drop the expectation that they will treat us any differently, will we actually be able to walk in the freedom of forgiveness.

Now read how the Lord began to rebuild Rocky and LuAnn's relationship:

A supernatural thing began to happen. As I sat there, I began to experience the living reality of my salvation: Christ living in me. Two thousand years ago this iniquity had been laid on Jesus and this very guilt had been covered with His blood. Two thousand years later Jesus wanted the forgiveness He had already purchased to flow through me to Rocky.

As I allowed that to happen, I had a strange and very real sensation that I had been given the greatest gift my husband could ever give me. For the first time in our marriage I had my husband. He was no longer loyal to himself or another woman. He cared only to be obedient to God and loyal to me. No human counselor had prompted Rocky's confession. He had never told anyone, until now.

<u>The</u> Counselor, the Holy Spirit, had convicted him. In a time of great pain, I felt the sweetness of Rocky's love for me as I had never known it before.

The Lord also convicted me that I should confess to Rocky my unfaithfulness before we had been married. This was a very humbling time for both of us as we walked in obedience to the Lord. We confessed our disobedience to the Lord in many things. We prayed together and asked the Lord, in the name of Jesus, to break all the sexual bonds in each of our lives from the past. As we obeyed God, the walls of fear, pride, judgment and control crumbled. The Lord moved through our marriage and made the two, one.

Healing is a process. There are good days when I walk after the spirit and allow the Lord to live and forgive through me. There are days when my flesh wins and I listen to the lies of the enemy. But the Lord has shown me that healing would come as I renewed my mind with the truth, God's truth. Rocky is a child of God. Rocky is the very righteousness of God in Christ. He is God's workmanship. He has the very nature of God. The Lord allowed me to see Rocky through His eyes. **Therefore from now on we (LuAnn) recognize no man (Rocky) according to the flesh** (2 Corinthians 5:16).

I also realized that I had been commanded to forgive as Christ had forgiven me. In <u>Love, Acceptance and Forgiveness</u>, Jerry Cook says, "Forgiveness involves forgetting. We have not truly forgiven someone until that matter is dismissed by us not to be retained anymore." We don't need to forget the learning and growth we gained from the experience, only the pain that pierced the heart. This is possible because Christ living in me has already forgiven and forgotten.

By experiencing God's love and forgiveness of us, we were able to give forgiveness, seek forgiveness, and begin rebuilding our relationship.

Rocky and LuAnn began to experience the dynamic, living reality of Christ as life. They began to love and live in the freedom that forgiveness brings. But it all started with the realization that God is God and they are not.

The story has a wonderful ending:

Rocky and I, after finishing our training, spent some time at our home back in Texas. But we had been so moved and so changed by our experiences at VCL International that we soon returned to Phoenix so that we both could work with VCLI to continue their work.

We truly have experienced our lives becoming one. We were unable to bear children, but the Lord has now blessed us with the birth of our first baby. This is a wonderful physical illustration of our emotional and spiritual oneness.

A few years earlier we adopted a beautiful little girl, Stephanie, who now has the little baby sister she prayed for. The Lord certainly knows how to cap His story. Her name is Emily and she is a perfect result of our independence turned to oneness. The Lord has literally made one from two.

* * *

The first scriptural truth to embrace before true forgiveness can happen is that God is God and we are not.

John grasped truth. Rocky and LuAnn grasped truth. Will you grasp it, too? To have the freedom to love and live again through the power of forgiveness, you must understand that God is God and you are not. Godship is the root of all offenses. You cannot continue to play God in your life and ever hope to experience the freedom of forgiveness.

But there is more truth to be grasped. To be able to love and live again, you must experience the depth of Christ's incredible love. To help you do this, let us seek some understanding of how the Lord demonstrated His matchless love for us.

The next chapter is the cornerstone of this book. Find out who and what empowers us to be able to live this incredible life of Christ.

Summary of Chapter Five

1. In order to be free to love and live through the power of forgiveness, there are scriptural truths that must be embraced.
2. One truth to embrace is that God is God and we are not. When we try to play god, it will always bring about a need to forgive.
3. We will only be able to forgive when we take responsibility for our own actions and attitudes.

Chapter Six

Jesus: The Power Source to Forgive

(Story told by Sharon)

You have come to the most important chapter of this book. What you discover here is the most profound thing any person can ever know: JESUS IS THE ANSWER. It is the Lord Jesus Christ who enables you to forgive others and live an abundant, overflowing life. It is Jesus who came to earth to be the model forgiver. It is the Lord Jesus who provides the love and life to your mortal souls and bodies. If Jesus is not the flaming passion of your life, you are empty and unable to love and live in freedom.

Do you think John has an understanding of Jesus as the answer? What about Rocky and LuAnn? To tell what kind of tree you are seeing, take a look at the tree's fruit. John's life, as well as Rocky and LuAnn's, now bear the fruit of love, joy, peace, and contentment. They know a depth of God's love that they could not have known without the trials they faced.

Understanding God's complete love and forgiveness of you is essential in allowing you to pass on that love and forgiveness to others. Sharon's life exhibits the fruit of Christ also. In fact, I don't know many people who are any more overwhelmed with God's love, grace, and mercy than Sharon.

I spent most of my life living in sadness, anxiety, fear, and depression, wanting to die because I thought something was wrong with me. I thought I was crazy or mentally impaired. I just couldn't quite seem to "get it." Whatever "it"was.

I grew up in an alcoholic home that was very abusive. My father was a bartender. He often stayed away from home for days at a time and cheated on my mom. He was so abusive that my mom couldn't take it. We moved one night while my dad was at work. I was happy in a way, but I also felt betrayed. A new house, a new school, and no friends.

The Freedom to Love and Live Again

My dad eventually found us, and came in the middle of the night and started beating my mom and trying to push her eyeballs out with his thumbs. I was frozen with fear. Mom tried to get her gun, but couldn't. She finally got away and ran outside.

Before I was eight, my friend's brothers molested me. It scared me. I did not understand what was going on, but I remember thinking, "This is what my father is doing with other women." By the age of eleven I was drinking, smoking pot, experimenting with other drugs, and having sex with boys. I was trying desperately to fit in somewhere. Looking back, I realize I was very angry and hurt. But I kept everything inside, trying not to let anyone know the real me.

Later, my mom and her boyfriend got a house together and we all moved in. I wish I could say we lived happily ever after, but hard times were just beginning. My mom and stepfather drank a lot and had brutal fights. Seeing blood and violence was normal. I usually ran to my room when my stepfather came home. One night he came home drunk, entered my room, and molested me. I was petrified.

I began running away from home, doing drugs and living at friends' homes. I was looking to something to fill the deep void I had in my life. Nothing seemed to fill it.

Sharon was desperate to be free. Did running away from home set her free? How about drugs? Did friends bring her freedom and fill the void in her life? No. Nothing but forgiveness of those who have wronged her will give Sharon the freedom she strives for.

But remember, there are truths to be grasped before forgiveness can happen. One truth is that we cannot play god and enjoy freedom. The second is that God's love and forgiveness of us enables us to forgive others. If Sharon is to forgive, she must realize what Christ has done to prove His love, and what He enables her to do because of His love.

Let's follow her story:

Eventually my parents could not handle me any more. They placed me in a psychiatric hospital. Once I got out, I returned to my patterns of running away and doing drugs. Still in search of something to fill the void, I resorted to living on the streets, selling my body for a bed to sleep in, a meal to eat or drugs to take. I wanted to die, so I tried suicide. The next few years were filled with parties, rapes, accidents, and abuse from boyfriends.

Finally, I got a job and started putting my life in order, or so I thought. I moved in with the man I would marry four years later. I was afraid that if I gained weight he would not love me any more, so I became anorexic and bulimic. I lived in fear and anxiety. I also had an abortion.

Then, I thought I figured out what I needed to make life complete. I got pregnant, then married, and we had a son whom I loved very much. "Okay," I thought, "life is full now." But it wasn't. My husband had affairs, so I retaliated by having my own affair and leaving him. We eventually got divorced and he went to jail on drug charges.

I was forced to work two full-time jobs to support my son and me, so I was very tired, angry and depressed. Life still wasn't full.

Then, my son contracted a rare virus and died at two years of age. I was in pain and cried out to God, "Why?" I hated God for that and blamed Him for taking the one thing I loved more than anything else in the world. So, it was back to drugs.

Meanwhile, I stole over $10,000 from an employer to help support my drug habit. On drugs, I became so paranoid I could not go outside or answer the phone. Miraculously, though, I ended up in church one day, high on crystal and coke, and heard the Gospel. I accepted Christ with my whole heart, not knowing what all that meant.

Who was this Christ that Sharon accepted? It is through Him that God made His unmatched love and forgiveness known and available. Jesus said to His disciples, *"He that has seen me has seen My Father"* (John 14:9b). Jesus was before Abraham (John 8:58). Jesus is the always existing God, the Eternal One. He is described by the apostle John in Revelation 1:13-18: *And in the middle of the lampstands one like a son of man, clothed in a robe reaching to the feet, and girded across His breast with a golden girdle. And His head and His hair were white like white wool, like snow; and His eyes were like a flame of fire; and His feet were like burnished bronze, when it has been caused to glow in a furnace, and His voice was like the sound of many waters. And in His right hand He held seven stars; and out of His mouth came a sharp two-edged sword; and His face was like the sun shining in its strength. And when I saw Him, I fell at His feet as a dead man. And He laid*

His right hand upon me, saying, "Do not be afraid; I am the first and the last, and the living One; and I was dead, and behold, I am alive forevermore, and I have the keys of death and of Hades."

Jesus is described again in Revelation 19:11-16: *And I saw heaven opened; and behold, a white horse, and He who sat upon it is called Faithful and True; and in righteousness He judges and wages war. And His eyes are a flame of fire, and upon His head are many diadems; and He has a name written upon Him which no one knows except Himself. And He is clothed with a robe dipped in blood; and His name is called The Word of God. And the armies which are in heaven, clothed in fine linen, white and clean, were following Him on white horses. And from His mouth comes a sharp sword, so that with it He may smite the nations; and He will rule them with a rod of iron; and He treads the wine press of the fierce wrath of God, the Almighty. And on His robe and on His thigh He has a name written, "KING OF KINGS, AND LORD OF LORDS."*

What makes Him so incredible? Jesus was the third person of the trinity with God the Father, who created the world (Genesis 1:26), and with the Holy Spirit. They had a relationship of perfect love without the imperfection of human selfishness or sin. They enjoyed all the wonders of being eternally holy and righteous in person and practice. They hated sin and all the rebellion and death it brought in the lives of the human race. As God, Jesus enjoyed all the peace and joy of the Godhead as a daily, eternal experience.

According to Philippians 2:5-8, Jesus voluntarily chose to leave all the pleasures of the godhead to take upon Himself the form of a man. He made Himself of no reputation. He became a slave of men, humbling Himself, even accepting the death that was due to men, simply because of His great longing and desire to have them restored back to God, His Father. God is not only loving, but also holy and righteous in character. He required death for the sin and rebellion of those living independently of Him (Romans 3:23, 26).

Well, consider this. To save the human race, Jesus had to pay the debt we could not pay so that the justice of a holy God could be satisfied. Only a righteous life could pay the debt of sin. The life of an imperfect sinner would never do. Jesus was the only perfectly righteous life that could pay the debt.

Born of a virgin, He lived in poverty, without social prestige. As God, He dumfounded the religious leaders, walked on water, hushed the raging seas, multiplied loaves and fish, and healed physical bodies without medicine. Yet this same loving, merciful Jesus took our sin upon Himself, paying the penalty of death for our sin. The perfect and holy One became sin for us, the acceptable sacrifice of the sins of the world. He took upon Himself my sins, your sins, past, present, and future. The Bible says that Jesus went into the pits of hell.

The pain that Jesus experienced to make forgiveness possible was made worse by the tragedy of the ungrateful human race. To be forgiven, and to make it possible for us to forgive, Jesus had to be severed from His eternal, intimate, loving relationship with His Father.

As Jesus entered the garden the night before His death He pleaded with His Father. He asked His Father again if the cup (death, by the shedding of His blood) could be halted. His Father insisted the only way you and I could be forgiven is through the shedding of blood of the perfect sacrifice. As the reality of this began to grip Jesus' heart, mind, and emotions, He began to agonize. Terror filled Him as He thought what it would be like not to be in sweet communion with His Father. That was the only thing He had ever known. As His joy turned to grief and His peace turned to sorrow, He began to sweat His own blood. The agony of the awareness of His Father turning His back on Him was so intense His human body began to bleed from His pores.

The human race accused Him and condemned Him for having done nothing but compassionate acts, healing people's bodies, hearts, and minds. But that condemnation was nothing compared to His Father condemning Him for our sins. As we tied His healing hands and smote His loving face beyond recognition, and as we lashed Him with leather thongs with shards of glass and metal, He never reviled us, but asked His Father to forgive us. As we crowned His royal head with an acacia bush crown, with thorns like needles about three inches long, He silently took what we all deserve for our selfish, self-centered, sinful lives. Now with His face, head and back bleeding, we mocked Him like a criminal, forcing Him to carry the cross we deserve.

We hear His cry, "My God, My God, why hast thou forsaken me?" **His Father has forsaken Him for <u>our</u> sake.** Jesus didn't have to die. He had the power to stop all this before it happened. He had the ability to heal. He had the resources of the universe available to Him, but He gave up His Spirit willingly for us, the just for the unjust, the sinless for the sinner, the holy for the unholy, so we could be forgiven once and for all. He died so we could be forgiven. He forgave so we could forgive just as He does.

Fortunately, Jesus didn't stay in the grave. Now, because of His resurrection, His life giving Spirit indwells those who accept the gift of Jesus' sacrifice. The Holy Spirit, who only indwells those who become believers, energizes us to forgive as Jesus forgave.

Did Sharon know that kind of love? What allowed her to forgive, rather than running to escape the pain of others? She needed to know the depth of God's love.

To appreciate His great love for us even more, consider what He went through before the final act of death. He chose to be born of a woman, to be dependent on humans as a baby. He was born in a stable made for animals. He lived in obscurity without wealth or social influence. He ultimately had no home to call His own. He was willing to be despised, rejected and considered a criminal. Isaiah 53:3 says, *He was despised and forsaken of men, A man of sorrows, and acquainted with grief; And like one from whom men hide their face, He was despised, and we did not esteem Him.*

He was completely misunderstood. There was gossip about His birth. He was condemned for doing good works on the Sabbath. He was ridiculed for socializing with prostitutes, tax collectors, and sinners. His disciples even rebuked Him for His commitment to die for them. They deserted Him when He needed them most.

The religious community sentenced Him to death. He was sold by one of His disciples for 30 pieces of silver. He was beaten physically to the point of near death, then forced to carry His own cross. They nailed His hands and feet with large nails, pierced His side with a spear, and gave Him vinegar to drink.

But here is the important part for Sharon, and for you to know. The pain He felt physically and emotionally paled in comparison to the terrible pain He felt in His heart. Why? Because the precious human beings He created for an intimate relationship with Himself don't recognize and accept the sacrifice He was paying to satisfy the holy justice of God. We still don't readily accept the pure gift of His death, so we continue the tragedy. That sacrificial death was sufficient for all mankind. The only requirement God has for us is to accept the gift of His Son and say thank you.

While Jesus hung on the cross for us, He continued to plead with His Father to forgive us for what we did to Him! Yes, "we" did it. And we still do it. He offered His love and forgiveness to us on the cross, yet we fail to accept it. No wonder forgiveness is such a difficult thing for us to give.

Without Christ, the concept of forgiveness we illustrate by the testimonies in this book would not be possible. Because of Jesus, we can now experience forgiveness <u>first</u> from Christ, <u>then</u> with each other. Jesus had to become sin and die for us to be able to forgive. Praise God, the sin stayed buried, but the Sin-bearer arose!

Sharon searched desperately in this world to find something to fill the void. She dipped into the eternal supply of God's love when she received Christ that day. The Lord began a process in Sharon's life that culminated with forgiveness. But the process started by Sharon recognizing the depth of God's love and forgiveness of her.

After another bout with depression, a friend invited me to a VCL Conference that changed my life. I had known the Lord for five years, but I was still a "baby" Christian. The scriptural concepts were new to me. One concept was forgiveness. Other counselors had tried to teach me to "forgive myself." But I cannot forgive myself! I am not Christ and I did not shed any blood. Besides, my blood is not powerful enough to forgive my sins. But Christ's blood is! I simply need to accept His forgiveness! The Bible says no one can forgive sin but God alone. (Romans 5:9-11, Mark 2:7)

I also discovered that Christ is in me and I am in Him. I am His child and He loves me as He does His Son, Jesus.

Having been empowered by His forgiveness, I made long lists of those who had hurt me, and those I had wronged, and I gave and asked forgiveness from them.

One of the most exciting examples is when I went to the former employer to confess stealing the $10,000. I knew I could go to jail, but I also knew it was the right thing to do. Humbly, I admitted taking the money, and I asked his forgiveness. After he said yes he also agreed to forgive my debt. By the grace of God, I did not go to jail, and I was not required to repay the debt.

I also gave forgiveness to the boys who molested me, my father who abused me and my mother, my stepfather who abused me sexually, my husband who was unfaithful to me, and all those who raped me.

The power of God's love and forgiveness made it possible for Sharon to forgive others. But that isn't the end of Sharon's story. When a person is free to love and live again, it has a profound effect on others. Read on.

Only a short time ago I found out my father lived just a few miles from me. I had not had contact with him since I was 10, but when I found out that he had had a stroke and was fighting cancer I set out to find him. I wanted to ask his forgiveness for not helping him when he was in need. I also wanted to tell him about Christ. No matter what anyone has ever done to me, I do not want them to spend eternity in hell. I asked the Lord for the right opportunity, and I got it.

I called my father to ask if I could come over. He said yes, and when I arrived we greeted each other with tears in our eyes. He looked different. The cancer was obviously serious. We talked for a while and I asked his forgiveness for many things. He forgave me and so did his wife. He even asked me for forgiveness and I forgave him. Finally, I was free, and so was he.

Physically, he began to go downhill. One day I went to see him and asked, "Dad, have you accepted Christ as your savior?" and "Do you know what that means?" He said no, that he was afraid because of all the terrible things in his life. I got to share with him how much God loves him, and offers forgiveness to him if he would only accept it. I told him that God's love and forgiveness is what enabled me to forgive. Then I said, "Dad, I haven't gotten to spend much of my earthly life with you, but I do want to spend eternity with you." He told me not to give up on him, and to keep praying for him.

The next day he had a seizure and I thought he was dying. When he finally came out of it he motioned for me to come close. He said, "I did it. I prayed." What joy! We will now spend eternity together.

He died a few days later, but I am rejoicing that I will spend forever with him. I am convinced that humble forgiveness of him brought him to the point of receiving God's forgiveness.

The wonderful story of forgiveness continues. After many years of praying for my sister, she accepted Christ with me while sitting in my car. I believe that she, too, saw true forgiveness in me. She saw that no matter what she has done to me, or what we went through, I still loved, accepted and forgave her. Now I get to spend eternity with her, too.

Everything I went through in my life was worth it so that I could understand Christ's love and forgiveness for me, so that I can pass it on to others.

* * *

I have come that you might have life and have it abundantly (John 10:10). Isn't that what most people in the world are looking for? When people become Christians, they do not change in their desire to have abundant life. Sharon knew the Lord Jesus as Savior, but was never discipled. She began to learn how to live. Her life became so transformed that today she works full-time on our staff at VCL International, helping other people put their lives together.

Sharon shared Christ's love and forgiveness with her ex-husband while he was in jail. After he got out, he also went through counseling, and is now in training himself to begin helping people put their lives back together. Sharon has the opportunity daily to show other people how to forgive, and who the One is that empowers it. She was aware of her lack of power to forgive, and that she did not even have the power to change her life patterns.

To fully understand the mechanics of forgiveness, it is important to see forgiveness from GOD'S point of view. God solved the problem of godship that started in the garden with Adam and Eve. He also solved the problems created among the human race due to godship. He made it possible not only through His divine forgiveness, but through human forgiveness, to heal the hurts and wounds created by man's sin.

Before we teach you the mechanics of forgiveness, we must show you how to let Christ Jesus empower you. That forgiveness is available to anyone willing to receive it.

LuAnn, John and Sharon shared about their perceived need for identity or significance. It is pretty hard to feel significant about yourself in experiences like John's or Sharon's. Yet, even in LuAnn's measure of success and good looks, she was empty, needing acceptance. There seems to be something missing on the inside of most people, even the ones with all the external trappings of this world's goods and blessings.

Each of these people came for help in their own particular situation of need. They all needed the same thing from God in order for them to experience and enjoy the benefits of freedom from their hurts. They all needed the power to forgive and to love the ones who had hurt or wounded them.

The first thing God did for mankind to experience supernatural life here on earth was to fix their broken, separated relationship with Him. To accomplish that He had to forgive man for violating Him and His standards. God, in His holiness and justice, is not one to overlook the wrong done by those He created. So, He sent His Son Jesus Christ to die and pay the requirement He established for man's sin. The only payment God decided to accept for sin was sacrificial death, and that sacrifice had to be perfect. An unrighteous sacrifice was not sufficient. The only one worthy enough for God's acceptance as payment for all of mankind's unrighteousness was the life of His own Son. His death accomplished that payment.

But He accomplished something even more incredible. His resurrection made it possible to give His resurrected life to us. The mystery of the gospel is Christ in you, living His life.

It was coincidental that, as I finished editing Sharon's story this week, I went to her home to celebrate the dedication of her new home to the Lord. This is the first home she has ever owned. As she called to confirm my arrival time, she said again:

I'm so overwhelmed with the grace of the Lord that He would forgive me for all that I did. I still find it hard to believe that I could have this beautiful home. I'm single, living on faith support. From all financial and human reason this is impossible. The Lord is soooo good to me!

God states clearly in His Word that there is only one purpose for mankind, and that purpose is the same, whatever our sex, our age, our nationality, or our status in life. In the Old Testament, He says He requires us to fear Him, to love Him, and to walk in all His ways (Deuteronomy 10:12). In the New Testament, He says we should love Him with all our heart, soul, mind and strength. God created all things for His pleasure (Revelation 4:11). It is in doing His will that we are completely fulfilled. We will experience a gnawing emptiness until the life of Christ becomes ours.

Because no human seeks after God (Romans 3:11), but seeks his own way (Job 21:14,15), man lost his original divine purpose of life. So God, because of the greatness of His love, paid the ultimate penalty to provide a way for man (who has free will to reject Him) to humble himself and come back to the beautiful, loving relationship with God that he had in the beginning.

Just because a believer has the Holy Spirit doesn't mean they have learned how to appropriate the life of Christ as Sharon did. The following chapters will not only demonstrate how to forgive, but also how to have the power of Christ to forgive as He forgave. Without the life of Christ as a living experience, one's ability to truly forgive as Christ forgave is impossible. To forgive seven times seventy takes divine power. Jesus is that power!

Sharon was able to forgive all the terrible tragic things done to her because of the incredible grace of Jesus' gift, and because she has His life to empower it. It wasn't just from knowing all the specifics described in the next chapters. The healing doesn't have to take years unless someone is trying to work out the hurt of their past through man-made methods or philosophies. In fact, the ones caught in that web seem to go on for years, never really being completely and totally healed and restored in the relationships that were broken. If you feel worn out or exhausted from the process, true forgiveness has not taken place. It may be necessary to go back to the previous chapters and face the issues of godship and discover the supernatural healing power that comes from Christ making you whole. The next chapter will tell you how to receive Christ's life and power, before learning the steps of forgiveness in a later chapter.

Summary of Chapter Six

1. It is only the all-powerful, supernatural life of Christ that enables us to forgive. Methods, philosophies, or even steps to forgiveness will fail without the empowering life of Jesus Christ.
2. In order to be free to love and live through the power of forgiveness, there are scriptural truths that must be embraced.
3. One such truth to embrace is that God loves and forgives us to a depth we cannot even conceive.
4. To be free to love and live again, we must plunge ourselves into the depth of God's love and forgiveness of us.

Chapter Seven

Thank You For Raping Me

(Story told by Lisa and Sharon)

Does God <u>really</u> cause all things to work together for good? What about when an innocent child is run over by a drunk driver? What about when a stray bullet pierces the skull of someone who happens to be in the wrong place at the wrong time?

Does God <u>really</u> expect us to give forgiveness to those drunk drivers and careless drive-by shooters? Is it even possible?

Certain truths must be realized for true forgiveness to result in the freedom to love and live again. Two of those important truths were discussed in Chapters Five and Six: a person must understand they cannot play god, and a person must appropriate the love and forgiveness of God before they can offer it to others. The third truth to embrace is that God is absolutely sovereign. Everything that happens is allowed by God for His glory and our benefit.

True freedom will never be realized until these three truths are experienced in your life. Lisa is totally free to love and live again. Let's find out why.

When I was 18 years old, I almost married my high school sweetheart, but realized it wasn't right so we called it off. I believed that the first person I was involved with sexually would be the last person I was ever with, or I would burn in hell. So, when I rebounded into another sexual relationship with a man 20 years older, I thought I was doomed.

I became a topless dancer for about ten years and met the nicest man I ever knew. He was fun and he made me laugh. He was told by doctors that he would die in a few years, crippled from Lou Gehrig's disease. He had dreams of being in the music industry and I thought I could help him achieve that. I backed him financially in his quest, but lost all the financial resources I had. We had lived together about 6 years before the doctors told him he had one year to live, so we decided to have a baby.

Our little boy still had his father two years later. We didn't know why he was still alive, but we were grateful. However, after further testing, we discovered he had a rare form of muscular dystrophy, not Lou Gehrig's disease. He could live to be 75 years old, but would continue to become more crippled. I worked three jobs because he was disabled.

"Great," I thought. "God is punishing me, and this is what is in store for me." I became desensitized and built up resentment towards God for allowing this to happen, and towards this man because I felt trapped. In depression, he turned to drugs. I used my money and my abilities to help him, but nothing helped. I felt guilty for wanting to leave, I felt guilty for the situation I had entered into, and I felt guilty for repeating the cycle of immorality rather than breaking it. I continued to believe God was punishing me.

Finally, at 28, I thought I was short-changing my son, so I became selfish. Motherhood was very important to me and I viewed this relationship as something that held me back. I took my son and left.

That created an opportunity for me to really think about my life. I had a horrible history of drugs and living immorally with men. I wanted to break free. I realized that I had done many wrong things that resulted in a lot of pain. I decided to clean up my act, but it didn't really work.

I didn't date much, but I started socializing with a man I had been a friend with before. He had been married and divorced five times, but he was able to offer me financial security. He had some good characteristics and I wanted to do what was best for my son and me. We agreed to abstain from sex because that was important to both of us.

One night we went to a restaurant owned by friends of mine. My friends treated me to a huge drink that I drank with dinner. Mixed with some medication I was taking, the drink was potent and I lost my senses. The events after dinner became a blank and I had no recollection of anything until the next morning. Because of our verbal agreement not to be sexually involved, I trusted this man, but was taken advantage of. He raped me that night.

Anger rose within me and I said many mean things to him. I didn't want to talk to him. I didn't want to see him. I didn't want anything to do with him. I threatened him and did many terrible things. In fact, I was determined that if he showed up at my place of work, I would report him to the police.

Where was God in all this? How could He allow all these horrible things to happen?

* * *

When we don't understand the biblical truth that God is absolutely sovereign, we wonder the same thing. Without that reality, it is impossible to forgive. Lisa needed to know about God's sovereignty, and about His love. She needed to understand why God allows problems.

My days are filled with listening to and helping people deal with the problems in their lives. Our own personal problems seem to be the worst ones because they affect us the most. People tend to blame God for those problems, just as Lisa did. In fact, it has become a popular teaching among Christian teachers, pastors, and counselors that there is a need to forgive God.

I have to ask the question, "What has God ever done wrong that He needs our forgiveness?" Often, I hear responses such as, "What about the poor, innocent babies that die of starvation? God could stop that if He wanted. Isn't that God's fault?"

To understand why forgiving God is impossible you must discover who God says He is and what right He has to do what He does. You also must understand His righteousness.

In a society that is always talking about it's rights, it is interesting how little or no consideration is given by mankind, including Christians, as to what God's rights are. What does God have to say about His rights, and why can He claim to have them? In determining if we need to forgive God, let's consider a few facts about man.

As man contemplates who God is, he does so with limited knowledge. Because of man's limited knowledge, he needs to receive the revelation from someone who has all knowledge. God's knowledge and character are revealed in and through the

Bible, which many so-called Christians do not even consider authoritative.

Not only is man limited in knowledge, but also in experience, due to a life-span that is limited to about 80 years (I Chronicles 29:15). God has an unlimited time span that has no beginning and no end. Yet, man in his limited awareness does not want to consider what the Almighty, Eternal, All-knowing God says.

Man is also limited in his resources to control life and circumstances. John, LuAnn, and Sharon all tried, but it never worked. They couldn't make things happen the way they wanted. The wealthiest billionaire cannot control whether he will die in a plane crash, a car accident, or natural death. Man is at the mercy of God's natural and spiritual laws.

In contrast, consider God as described in Acts 17:24-25: *The God who made the world and all the things in it; since He is Lord of heaven and earth, does not dwell in temples made with hands; neither is He served by human hands, as though He needed anything, since He Himself gives to all life and breath and all things.* God created all things and has ultimate authority over all things. *"He who comes from above is above all, he who is of earth is from the earth and speaks of the earth. He who comes from heaven is above all"* (John 3:31). *For by Him all things were created, both in the heavens and on earth, visible and invisible, whether thrones or dominions or rulers or authorities—all things have been created by Him and for Him. He is also head of the body, the church; and He is the beginning, the first-born from the dead; so that He Himself might come to have first place in everything* (Colossians 1:16, 18).

Man is confused when he considers God to be no more than like himself. God is above all. He has the right to do whatever He chooses with His creation, and He is totally righteous in everything He does. If God chose to send me to hell after saving me, indwelling me with His Spirit, and giving me the righteousness of Himself, He could do so and it would be right. He is God and can do whatever He pleases. Who are we to tell God what He can or cannot do?

It is ludicrous to even consider that we would ever need to forgive God when He has never done anything wrong. How could we, the created beings with limited abilities, knowledge, resources, life span, and awareness evaluate whether God was wrong anyway?

* * *

So what does God have to say about problems in our lives? Romans 8:28 says, *And we know that God causes all things to work together for good to those who love God, to those who are called according to His purpose.* Is He able to work all things together for good in Lisa's life? If so, and she realizes that, what effect will it have on relationships in her life? Let's find out.

A co-worker of mine was my role model. I was at peace when I was around her, because the peace of the Lord oozed out of her. She always found time for me, and she prayed for me. That was a new concept to me. I admired her and wanted what she had.

Following the rape, I was encouraged to go for counseling. I chose to go to VCL International rather than deal with it through secular counselors. I finally opened up to my counselor about the events of my life, and she sensed a need in my life. She introduced me to Jesus Christ! I did not go there seeking to become a Christian, I went there to fix things in my life. But I realized, without Christ, my problems would never be fixed. I was so excited to have what my coworker had.

In counseling, I learned about God's love and forgiveness of me for all the wrong choices I make. I also learned that I cannot be god of my life. I cannot make my life work like I want it to work. That requires that I trust the sovereignty of God. He allowed all the things in my life for a reason. I may never know all the reasons, but I do know He is sovereign. Because I began to understand His sovereignty, I began to forgive the people in my life who had hurt me. For the first time in my life I was set free from the humiliation, betrayal and emotional anguish.

I chose to step beyond giving forgiveness to actually rebuilding torn relationships appropriately. I believed the man who raped me was truly sorry for what he had done and we saw each other as friends on a safeguarded basis. He knew that I was devoting my life to Jesus, but he never made that transition. I knew I could not marry someone who was not a Christian, but I loved him as one of God's creations.

I tried a number of times to explain to him how God could carry the weight of it all and that he didn't have to. There was a time I told him indirectly that I thought I should thank him for that situation. I said that because I wanted to show him that I was free and that he could give that burden to God like I had. I assured him that he did not have to let it be so heavy, but he missed the point. I don't think, to this day, he really knows what it means to have the burden of that sin lifted off of him.

What Satan meant for evil, God used for good. I realized that I had found new life in Christ because of this horrible incident. I became free from bondage as I forgave all the offenders in my life and learned that God is a very loving God, full of forgiveness, not punishment.

After all that, and after I had really come through this whole issue personally, I realized that because of him and because of the incident I had found new life. I indirectly said to him, "Thank you for raping me." God used that evil for His glory.

* * *

Lisa would not have been able to say thank you for what happened had we only shown her how to forgive. Some say forgiveness is simply a choice. But Lisa had something greater happening inside her that caused her attitude to change from anger to thankfulness for the violation that happened to her. That change was far superior to knowing and practicing forgiveness by choice. The dynamic of the new life in Christ made it possible to forgive "as Christ forgave."

Part of grasping the sovereignty of God is in experiencing that dynamic. It was that dynamic that made the impossible, possible. It is a supernatural work of the Lord Jesus Christ.

Lisa not only became a Christian, but was also shown how to appropriate and identify with the life of Christ so that forgiveness could be a lifestyle. Many Christians say they forgive, but continue to live in the same way as if they had not forgiven. This seems to stem from knowing only half the Gospel. They know Jesus died for them and forgave them of their sin, but they do not function according to the fact that He arose again so that they could love and live again.

Lisa learned that her past is not who she is. Many teachers and counselors today are pouring out "self-esteem" messages which encourage people to focus on self. Meaning and purpose in life do not come from the endless "positive mental attitude" statements repeated to one's self. Meaning and purpose flow from the life of Christ that focuses on death of our self-life.

Lisa learned that changing "bad" thoughts to "good" thoughts does **not work**. Changing "lies" to "truth" **does** work. *You shall know the truth, and the truth shall make you free* (John 8:32). The truths in the identity list at the end of this chapter illustrate the truths Lisa learned. Follow the instructions to appropriate them as Lisa did.

When she received Christ, Lisa inherited an entirely different past, the past of Christ Jesus. *I have been crucified with Christ; and it is no longer I who live, but Christ lives in me* (Galatians 2:20a). This makes it possible to discuss her old past objectively, without it destroying or upsetting her present life. All the wrong choices (sin) were nailed to Christ on the cross and delivered to eternal hell, so that she could experience abundant life in Christ Jesus.

If you do not understand the power of the cross in your life, you will not receive the abundance of God's love and forgiveness that enables you to love and forgive others. Do you know who you are in Christ?

Let's say you do not know that you are a member of the Rothschild or Rockefeller family. You are 45 years old, but have never known your heritage. Your name is on the birth certificate and they are your relatives, but you do not know that you are related. Would you be enjoying any of the privileges of their financial wealth? No. Would you like to enjoy it? It is yours to enjoy simply because of the benefit of your position by birth.

If you truly understood the practical benefits of the position as a member of God's family, it would change your life forever. It is easy to trust God and enjoy the privileges in His life if we know our position and what the privileges are. One of the privileges is a life of freedom that comes from giving and seeking forgiveness.

* * *

Having learned of God's sovereignty, the role that the cross played in her life, and the power of God's love, Lisa was able to say "thank you" for the results of being raped.

By the way, the friend that encouraged her and prayed for her during difficult situations was Sharon, who you read about in Chapter Six! Sharon learned the principle of God's sovereignty, then passed it along to Lisa. Here is what Sharon says about her circumstances:

You may say, "Some of that stuff should never have happened. Why should Sharon forgive when, as a little girl, she should not have grown up in a mess like that?" With the revelation of the Holy Spirit, I came to a conclusion: God is sovereign. (Isaiah 40:10-11) The sovereign Lord comes with power and He will gather me in His arms. God didn't do those horrible things. Depraved, sinful people did. God allowed that in my life because he gave mankind a free will. I believe that these things happened to glorify Him. He knows what is best for me. He protected me through all of it, even when I thought He wasn't there.

Yes, I was angry at God, but He was big enough to handle that and draw me into His lovingkindness. I poured my heart out to Him, I confessed that I thought I knew better than He did. Always gracious, God forgave me. Now I am able to forgive others "just as Christ forgave me."

It was Sharon's life, as much as her words, which had an impact on Lisa. Lisa learned about the life of Christ and the sovereignty of God by seeing Sharon actually live out those truths. As a result, Lisa caught the vision. She began to experience God's love and forgiveness. She began to give forgiveness to those who had wronged her, and she sought forgiveness from those whom she had wronged. The final phase of forgiveness is restoration of relationships. Lisa's relationship to the one who raped her was restored, just as John and Sharon were restored to their fathers.

What effect does that freedom have in Lisa's other relationships? Finish reading Lisa's testimony:

My son's life is now being positively affected. I explained to him how fortunate he is to be blessed with a Christian family. He is seven now and is all excited about Jesus. I walked the wrong way for 33 years, but my son has the privilege of being way ahead of his mom at his age. He is very much in touch with God. He prays when he has problems, and is learning about the sovereignty of God. He is being enabled to give forgiveness to those who could cause problems in his life.

My best friend is also being affected by my life. Her parents have been Christians for many years and she knows a lot about Christianity. She just isn't willing to become a Christian yet. However, since all this has happened to me, we have had some great conversations. She is also watching the life of Christ being exhibited in my life. I'm not perfect, but the grace of God is sufficient. He will use me, regardless of the mistakes I make, to influence my friend and draw her to Himself. I am confident that, some day, she will know the love of Christ.

* * *

We have seen how terrible things can happen because of the depravity of man exercising godship. This demands the need for forgiveness as an ongoing lifestyle. We are aware that these devices only put us in more bondage and result in broken relationships.

We now know that the power to truly forgive is not in methods, philosophies, or techniques, but in the life of Christ available to every believer. The stage is set. We will unravel the actual, practical, simple steps of the process of giving forgiveness in the next chapter. Later we will also explain the steps of seeking forgiveness and rebuilding broken relationships, which gives us the freedom to love and live again.

But keep in mind, it is not a set of steps that makes giving and seeking forgiveness happen. The steps are only a guide. The power to actually give and seek forgiveness is in Jesus Christ.

Summary of Chapter Seven

1. God is totally sovereign and can be trusted to cause all things to work together for His glory and our benefit.
2. When Christ's life was exchanged for ours, and we begin to function in the dynamic life of Christ, freedom is possible through forgiveness.
3. As we understand who God is and who He created us to be, we experience the depth of love and forgiveness that allows us to forgive others.
4. Our supernatural life of Christ will have major impact on the lives of others as we experience the freedom in forgiveness.

Thank You For Raping Me

Identity List

**The truest things about me are what God says about me
    (1 Corinthians 4:3-4).**
In Christ I am *a child of God—born of God* (John 1:12-13).
In Christ I am *being saved by His life* (Romans 5:10).
In Christ I am *free from condemnation* (Romans 8:1).
In Christ I am *an heir of God, joint heir with Christ* (Romans 8:17).
In Christ I am *a saint* (Romans 8:27).
In Christ I am *accepted* (Romans 15:7).
In Christ I am *a possessor of the mind of Christ* (1 Corinthians 2:16).
In Christ I am *a new creature* (2 Corinthians 5:17).
In Christ I am *the righteousness of God* (2 Corinthians 5:21).
In Christ I am *blessed with every spiritual blessing* (Ephesians 1:3).
In Christ I am *adopted as God's child* (Ephesians 1:5).
In Christ I am *God's workmanship created for good works* (Ephesians 2:10).
In Christ I am *a member of God's household* (Ephesians 2:19).
In Christ I am *a citizen of heaven* (Philippians 3:20).
In Christ I am *holy and blameless and beyond reproach* (Colossians 1:22).
In Christ I am *complete [perfect]* (Colossians 2:10).
In Christ I am *alive and forgiven of all my transgressions* (Colossians 2:13).
In Christ I am *a member of a royal priesthood* (1 Peter 2:9).
In Christ I am *a partaker of God's divine nature* (2 Peter 1:4).
In Christ I am *given eternal life today* (1 John 5:11-13).
In Christ I am *released from my sins* (Revelation 1:5).

RENEWING my mind brings about **TRANSFORMATION.**
And do not be conformed to this world, but be transofrmed by the renewing of your mind, that you may prove what the will of God is, that which is good and acceptable and perfect (Romans 12:2).

1. Read a verse listed above in its context and check cross references.
2. Report to God that I believe (adhere to, trust in, rely on) what He says about me is true.
3. Respond to God in prayer by thanking Him for what He did, "Father, I believe You when Your Word says I am a saint. I may not feel like one, but that's what You call me, so I believe it. Thank You!"—1 Thessalonians 5:18
4. Recognize what this verse teaches me about God and praise Him for who He is!
5. Reject my old view of myself. This would include no longer calling myself names like: failure, dummy, stupid, idiot, and loser. Also, I would stop seeing myself as: sinner, alcoholic, lazy, fornicator, homosexual, or liar.—1 Corinthians 6:9-11
6. Rejoice that my mind is being renewed each time I choose the truth.
7. Receive direction for today as a result of this verse. "Lord, I see what You have done and who You are, now what do You want me to do regarding this truth?"

The Freedom to Love and Live Again

Chapter Eight

How to Give True Forgiveness

In these days of casual relationships, many of us believe that forgiveness is an easy thing to come by. If someone comes to you and says, "I've been wrong, would you please forgive me for___ ?", what might you say?

"Sure, I forgive you. Why not?"

It seems like it should be that easy. But it isn't easy at all. It is impossible without Christ.

Remember John's story of the abuse he suffered at his father's hands? Would it seem easy for John to forgive his father for so many horrific transgressions? Without the supernatural power of forgiveness available from Christ it would be impossible. <u>With</u> that supernatural power, <u>anything</u> is possible.

What is the process of forgiveness that John followed? How did his life change from a wasteland to a garden? How could you use that process in your life to forgive your loved ones? Read on and you will discover the simple steps to true forgiveness.

WHAT GIVING FORGIVENESS IS NOT

Before we consider <u>how</u> to forgive, let's first clarify what forgiveness is and what it is not.

Forgiveness is <u>not</u> excusing a person. John could have easily said, "Sure, my Dad was very cruel to me but it was the result of how his Dad treated him. He never saw the example of a loving Father so how could I expect him to treat me in a loving way?'

While it may seem generous of John to excuse his father's behavior, excusing is not forgiving! To err is human, to excuse is normal, and to <u>forgive</u> is divine. Often, when we try to forgive our loved ones, particularly our parents, it is hard to admit they did anything wrong. "Hey, that's my Mother we're talking about, she did the best she could."

But to be able to forgive transgressions you must be able to see them clearly. We are not interested in condemnation, only a clear look at the truth. What is the goal of the forgiveness process? To get revenge or to hurt the person who hurt us? Of course not. We want to give forgiveness so that we will be free to relate to this person again. So, don't excuse—forgive.

If forgiveness requires a clear look at offenses, closing your eyes to those offenses isn't going to work either. Ignoring or tolerating transgressions will not free your soul to love your transgressor. How often we bury our heads in emotional sand, because it is so much easier than confronting the source of our pain: "Sure, my Dad was wrong in how he treated me, but I try not to think about it, I just put up with it for now." That is not forgiving!

Think about a person that you need to forgive. What is the truth about this person? Has he or she gossiped about you? Have they embarrassed or humiliated you? Trying to overlook, ignore, or tolerate the hurtful actions done to you will not work, and we all know it won't. The hurt will fester and grow. Face the hurt so that you can forgive it.

Let's consider the Biblical example of Joseph from the book of Genesis. Joseph was hurt by his brothers. He could have excused them saying, "Well, they are a rough bunch and I guess I bugged them with my dreams. Plus, they were probably jealous of Dad's treatment of me, so what could I expect?"

Genesis 50:17 is the first time the word "forgive" is used in the Bible. Joseph's brothers lie, telling him that their father, Jacob, has instructed Joseph to forgive his brothers for their cruel treatment of him. He had not excused his brother's actions.

In fact, Joseph has already forgiven them when he reveals himself to them and says, weeping loudly, *"I am Joseph, your brother, whom ye sold into Egypt. Now therefore be not grieved, nor angry with yourselves, that ye sold me hither: for God did send me before you to preserve life"* (Genesis 45:4b, 5 KJV).

Nor did Joseph exercise Godship, telling his brothers that he was in no position to judge them: *Do not be afraid, for am I in God's place?* (Genesis 50:19) Further, Joseph saw the truth of Romans 8:28 long before Paul wrote it. And as for you, you meant evil against me, but God meant it for good. (Genesis 50:20a) Joseph was a man who knew how to forgive.

WHY GIVING FORGIVENESS IS NECESSARY

We know in our heart of hearts that we must forgive. If we cannot we can only expect negative results:

1. You could continue to hold your offenders guilty. This can result in an accumulated treasure of fault that can be cashed in when you reach a breaking point. Remember John trading blows with his Dad for the first time in his life, and the police having to separate the two of them? That was a day when he cashed in his resentments.

2. Without forgiveness you can become a bitter person. Hebrews 12:15 states, *See to it that no one comes short of the grace of God; that no root of bitterness springing up causes trouble, and by it many be defiled.* As we will see, the issue of God's grace is at the heart of forgiveness.

3. When you don't forgive you secretly or maybe not so secretly want to see the offender get punished for his or her transgression. Proverbs 24:17-18 says, *Do not rejoice when your enemy falls, And do not let your heart be glad when he stumbles; Lest the Lord see it and be displeased, and He turn away His anger from him.*

4. Withholding forgiveness from one person may interfere with relationships with others. If I don't forgive you I may have trouble relating to another person who reminds me of you. Have you ever felt uncomfortable around someone and didn't know why? Perhaps that person reminds you of someone whom you have not forgiven.

   I remember discipling a man who had a real problem with his woman boss. For several sessions we discussed how he might forgive her, working through the steps you will see below. Yet he was still having problems with his boss. One day he lit up and exclaimed, "I know what's wrong, I have been forgiving the wrong woman. My boss reminds me of my mother who abandoned me when I was five years old. That's who I need to forgive."

God in Christ has freely forgiven you. This is the motive which should constrain you to forgive others. God's forgiveness toward you is free, it precedes even your repentance and is the cause of it. He forgave you far more than you can ever be called upon to forgive others.

One final thought on why you should forgive. It is commanded. Jesus in Mark 11:25 said, *"And whenever you stand praying, forgive."* That word "forgive" is in the imperative tense. It is a command.

WHAT HAPPENS IF I DON'T FORGIVE?
(I Am The Offended Diagram)

This diagram, found at the end of the chapter, points out what happens when you are offended. You create a court room scene in your mind and you are the judge. Whoever has offended you is handcuffed and stands condemned. You, as the judge, are issuing your sentence.

What's wrong with this picture? Simple: You and I can't be the judge. We are not qualified. James 4:12 states, *There is only one lawgiver and judge, the One Who is able to save and to destroy, but who are you who judge your neighbor?* We don't have the spiritual credentials to be a judge. God is without sin; we are not.

Psalm 9:8a says, *He will judge the world in righteousness.* Only God has the right to execute judgment. Our attempt to lay guilt on the offender by setting a standard is reacting after the flesh and exercising godship. Like irritable children we complain, "This person should not have treated me that way." That statement is so generic any offense could be included. What happens if we react after the flesh?

Something very surprising and dramatic! We, the judge, not the offender, are thrown into jail.

Look at the diagram, "The Result of My Fleshly Reactions".

This is the result of dishing out the sentence as the judge. We can punish with silence or wrath. We can give the offender a tongue lashing using abusive speech or swearing. Perhaps it would be fun to bring other people into the conflict by gossip or slander. None of these are the solution. They only imprison us in our own anger and frustration.

Instead of meting out our own justice we simply need to forgive. When? Ephesians 4:26b gives a clear time frame. *Do not let the sun go down on your anger.* Some people have misinterpreted this to say, "Stay up and fight all night!" If both people are dog-tired you may need to table the discussion until the next day, when bodies and minds are fresh. However, most often, conflict needs to be resolved quickly and forgiveness given.

I was counseling a couple over the phone about a current conflict that started several days ago. Conflicts were piled upon one another and none of them had been resolved. The wife finally said to her husband, "If you want a divorce, then go get it." When they finished talking, I asked each of them if they really wanted a divorce and they both said no. But here they were, discussing the dissolution of their marriage, simply because conflicts had piled upon one another without forgiveness or resolution. Believe me, the enemy works like this. He works at trying to drive people apart. We must solve the conflict quickly-the sooner, the better.

There is an interesting truth tucked away in Ephesians 4:27: *Do not give the devil an opportunity.* The NIV translates the word, "opportunity" as "foothold." In the Greek the word is "topos" from which we get our word "topography," which is a geographical location. So, if we don't forgive and we "let the sun go down on our anger," then we give the Devil a place to set up shop from whence he can further torment us.

Have you ever known a bitter person? So often people grow bitter simply because they will not or cannot forgive someone who has hurt them. See the bars in this diagram? This person is held prisoner by the sinful reactions he or she commits. By not forgiving the ramifications of the hurt, another bar is formed to hold this person fast in the prison of unforgiveness. We are actually held prisoner by reacting after the flesh.

"But," you say, "I'm simply waiting for them to admit they were wrong and to ask for my forgiveness." Well, we agree that the offender <u>should</u> ask for forgiveness, but what if they never do? Are you going to stay in this prison forever? You can only stop the Devil's torment and control of the flesh by giving your forgiveness. Look closely at the diagram and you will see the keys to freedom are in the prisoner's hands.

We were not intended to live in anger but in forgiveness. Anger, even if justified, is not to be cherished. Oswald Chambers says "If there is the tiniest grudge in your mind against anyone, from that second your spiritual penetration into the knowledge of God stops!"

ARE THERE PEOPLE YOU NEED TO FORGIVE?

As you have been reading, perhaps the Lord has brought people to your mind that you need to forgive. Why not make a list, right now, while you're thinking about it? Here are a few questions to help you:

1. Who is there in your life that generates anger, hurt, or bitterness when you think about them?
2. Who don't you like to hear spoken of favorably?
3. Who easily offends you on a regular basis?
4. Who would you like to see suffer financially, physically or a set back?
5. Who would you like to tell just how much they have hurt you?
6. Who has ruined your life?
7. Who has robbed or cheated you out of something you should have had. (Such as being robbed of your childhood, a happy home, a normal family or money in the bank?)
8. Who will you not associate with because he/she has hurt you or someone you love?
9. Who has hurt you so much that you feel angry or mistrustful towards God, feeling that He should have protected you from this person?

If you have made a list of names, then you will need to forgive these people. And remember, being bitter doesn't necessarily mean you scowl and say nasty things. It may simply mean that you have closed yourself off from relating to another person. Or, it may mean that you have difficulty being objective about a particular person. Whatever the case, you are not free in your life and relationships. God sincerely wants you to experience freedom. So you need to take an honest look inside to make absolutely sure that there is no "root of bitterness" in your soul. (Hebrews 12:15)

SO YOU THINK YOU'VE ALREADY FORGIVEN?

Many Christians think they have forgiven when, in fact, they haven't. Many think that it is spiritual to forgive. We want to look spiritual, even to ourselves, so we say the words, "Yes, I forgive you," or "Yes, I have forgiven him/her." But inside, we are still hurt, angry, resentful, bitter and/or ambivalent toward the person who has offended us.

There are only two possibilities here. The first is that we simply are angry. So we say that we forgive, thinking that we're going to convince God, ourselves, and everyone else. We convince ourselves that our anger is a righteous anger. Of course, in a year or so we end up with righteous ulcers or righteous divorces or righteous church splits.

The other possibility is that we do not understand how to forgive. There may be times when we fully intend to forgive but are unaware of the steps involved, or what forgiveness feels like when it is properly done.

When we don't understand how to forgive another person it is usually because we do not understand how God has forgiven us. *...forgiving each other, whoever has a complaint against anyone; just as the Lord forgave you, so also should you.* (Colossians 3:13)

Our need to forgive is not really between the offender and us. It is between God and us. God told us to do it, demonstrated how to do it, and provided the Life Source to do it. We have the ultimate forgiver living inside us.

Forgiveness is a choice of the will. Whenever God requires something He provides the resources to do it. I Thessalonians 5:24 is a wonderful promise, *Faithful is He that calleth you, Who also will do it.* (KJV) He has called us to be a forgiving people. He will also empower us to forgive as a way of life.

I had been a Christian a long time, but no one ever told me how to forgive. They told me I <u>should</u> do it, but I never saw <u>how</u> to do it until I came to understand these principles. There are books on the market that say that unless a person comes to you and asks you for forgiveness, you don't have to give it. I don't agree with them. Jesus says that if you have something against them, forgive them!

We've finally reached the steps to forgiveness we've been promising throughout this book. So let's see how you give true forgiveness!

WHAT IS GIVING FORGIVENESS?

Here are several factors in biblical forgiveness:

1. The whole concept and means of forgiving man's guilt was God's idea.

2. Forgiveness precedes even the repentance of the sinner. Remember what Jesus said, "Father forgive them..." They had not repented, but He had already asked the Father to forgive them.

3. Our guilt as sinners should not be overlooked or ignored or rationalized away. It has to be removed. This is why it is so important that when someone hurts you, that you forgive the offense, not just overlook it.

4. After forgiveness the formerly guilty are no longer guilty. This is extremely important. If you think, "They're still guilty, I've just forgiven them", then you have not understood or given true forgiveness.

HOW DO I PREPARE TO FORGIVE?

There are specific steps that the people in this book took as they prepared to forgive their loved ones. You must begin by taking the time to listen as God brings to your mind the names of those who have hurt you. Let's walk through the specific steps that John took as he prepared to forgive his father. The first step John took was to prepare four lists. These lists will help you to think through the forgiveness process slowly and thoroughly, making sure you are not missing anything:

1. List what this person did or didn't do that hurt you. John's list included such things as: humiliating him, criticizing him, forcing him to perform sexual acts, physical beatings, verbal abuse, not loving him with words or touch, and not showing him how to be a man.

2. List how you felt emotionally as a result of the hurts. John said he felt: humiliated, rejected, used, powerless, afraid, confused, and harassed.

3. List all the ramifications of the hurt. John's relationship with God was damaged because he prayed and still the sexual acts continued. This hurt his relationship with God, because John thought he could not trust God to protect

him when he needed it. Physically John suffered terribly, drinking and abusing drugs. His marriage was affected because he didn't want to relate sexually with his wife and because he fought with her for control of the marriage. He didn't have friends because he was afraid they would abuse him; he put up walls to protect himself from rejection and his relationships remained superficial. He worked long hours to succeed financially, thinking this would lead to acceptance. Finally, his role as a father was frustrating because of his terrible relationship with his own father. This list is very vital and seldom considered. Many times in counseling we see someone give forgiveness yet not experience freedom. Why? Because the act was forgiven but not all the serious and ongoing ramifications of the act.

4. List your sinful reactions. John's Dad may have been guilty of gross violations. However, John was not perfect. He physically attacked his Dad. He became very controlling and manipulative in relationships. He harbored a heart full of bitterness. We can understand how he could have these reactions, but we cannot excuse them. They must be a part of the forgiveness process as well.

You may think making these lists are too detailed or time consuming but they are important. Why try to do something as important as forgive your loved ones or friends, without considering these vital details?

Have you ever made a list to go to the store? Recently I made one, then left in at home as I ran out the door. When I returned from the store, I checked the list. I had forgotten three items and had to go back to the store. We often see people go too quickly through forgiveness then have to go back later to finish. Why? Because they thought they could save a little time by skipping the lists.

Once you have done this a few times you will become skilled at creating the four lists.

You will find blank lists to use in Appendix A at the end of this chapter. If you are forgiving someone for a single offense, some of these lists may not apply. For example, you may not have had time

71

to fire back a stinging comment or made some other sinful reaction. In fact, the quicker you give forgiveness the less time it takes.

HOW DO I ACTUALLY FORGIVE?

Look at the "I Choose To Extend Forgiveness" diagram at the end of this chapter.

Remember the keys we saw in the prisoner's hands in the earlier diagram? Now we can use them to get out of the jail of unforgiveness. By using these keys you will be set free from the prison and torment of unforgiveness. Now the truth about you can be seen and realized. Someone said as they looked at this diagram, "This must be a government lock, it takes seven keys to open it."

It may seem complicated at first, but remember how valuable our goal is: the total freedom that true forgiveness can bring. That's why we need to use all seven keys:

1. Examine your feelings and tell God how you feel. Psalm 62:8b says, *Pour out your heart before Me.* Tell God about this hurt and how you felt. Look at List 2, where you recorded all your feelings. God loves you and wants to hear how you feel.

2. Now admit to God that you have been holding the person guilty for the act (List 1), the hurt (List 2), and the ramifications of the offense (List 3). As you do this, read off in prayer to God all points on your lists. Pray with your eyes open and share with God all you wrote as you prepared to forgive. If other items come to your mind while you are praying, include them.

3. Now we come to the most important key - actually forgiving. Every time the Apostle Paul uses the word "forgive" in his epistles it is a combination of two words: Grace and to give. So, to forgive means to give grace to someone. Isn't that how we became Christians? God gave grace to us. Now we can return the favor, by extending or giving grace to another person. Colossians 3:13 explains, *Forgiving each other, whoever has a complaint against anyone.*

Now it is time to say to God that you give the offender the same grace God gave to you. You forgive for what was done, how

72

you felt, and all the ramifications. Once again you can read these off your lists or just mention the topics from your lists.

4. 1 Peter 3:7 says, *Casting all your anxiety upon Him, because He cares for you.* Now it is time to cast this person, the source of your anxiety, upon the Lord. In prayer tell God that you are putting this person into His hands and letting go. You will allow God to work in this person's life in His way and his time.

   Don't give God any advice at this point like, "Lord, I know how this person ought to act and how to treat me, so if You would like some inside scoop I'll be glad to fill You in on the details." Put the person into God's hands, let go, and let Him deal with them.

5. Now it's your turn. Pull out List 4. Read down the list and admit to God your sinful reactions. Confess to God that you were wrong. By confessing you are agreeing with God that you were wrong. You could also mention you were wrong for holding the person guilty. At this point if He shows you any other areas of godship admit them and receive His forgiveness. You don't have to beg God for forgiveness. Thank Him that Jesus already paid the price for your forgiveness and receive it with gladness.

6. Now you can choose to live in the new creation you are in Christ. Accept the fact that God has forgiven you. Lay aside your fleshly reactions.

7. Finally, tell God you are willing to be reconciled to the offender and allow God to love that person through you. God gave us the ministry of reconciliation in 2 Corinthians 5:18. If this person committed some crime against you or deeply hurt you then this is just the first step. The two of you would have to work together to rebuild trust.

* * *

After you finish praying through these seven keys ask yourself this question, "Is this person guilty now?" They may have been seen as guilty earlier, but now, because you have forgiven them, they are not guilty.

The Freedom to Love and Live Again

Praise God! They are free and so are you. This may look like a long process. Once you make up the four lists it only takes about 10 - 13 minutes to pray through these seven keys. Not much time invested to be free and obedient.

When you are finished giving forgiveness destroy all the lists. You are now free to live in the present, not the past. Do not tell the person you have forgiven them. They may not see any need to be forgiven. Don't call your Father and say, "Hey Dad, I just read this book on forgiveness and I took the time to forgive you." You may hear a gasp and then he may say, "What, you forgave me? What did I need to be forgiven for? You were the child I bent over backward for, I did everything for you and you never even had the courtesy to say thanks!"

If that does happen you will need to check the next chapter and see how to get forgiveness from your offended father. Sometimes after you have forgiven someone that person comes to you under the conviction of the Holy Spirit and seeks your forgiveness. What would you say? Don't say, "Well, I want you to know I have already forgiven you. I am so spiritual that I forgave you three weeks ago. I'm glad you are finally catching up to me." You didn't forgive them so that you could be holier-than-thou. You forgave them to be obedient to Christ and, as a result, set yourself free. Instead, try replying like this: "Sure, I'd be glad to forgive you. I thank God for your sensitive heart to His direction."

What happens if you give forgiveness to someone and you still feel upset or uncomfortable? It could be you were not specific enough. I remember one lady in counseling who forgave her husband for calling her names. It didn't feel finished. I told her to write out the names that he had called her and go through the process again. She listed names like, pig, witch, cow, and bitch. As she became more specific she felt finished.

Another reason you might feel hurt is that you have forgiven the offense but not all the ramifications. What was done long ago is still affecting you today. All of those ramifications must be forgiven.

WHAT HAPPENS AFTER I GIVE FORGIVENESS?

When John forgave his father he said that forgiveness included, "No longer holding a grudge, no longer having negative feelings, and no longer holding him guilty."

He now has a forgiving and loving relationship with his father. After all they went through, that is certainly a tribute to God's grace and the power of forgiveness. You can experience that change in your life as well. Who is it that keeps coming to your mind that you know you need to forgive? Take the time, make the time, to give forgiveness to experience freedom.

HOW DO I KNOW IF IT WORKED?

After you have forgiven someone how do you know you really did it? Consider the following:

1. Are you sincerely able to thank God for the lessons learned during the pain (Romans 8:28-29)?
2. Can you talk about your hurt without getting angry, without feeling resentful and without the slightest thought of revenge (Ephesians 4:31)?
3. Are you willing to accept your part of the blame for what happened?
4. Can you revisit the scene or the person(s) involved in your hurt without experiencing a negative reaction?
5. Are you rewarding with good those who have hurt you (Romans 12:20-21)?

Notice that forgetting about the offense or the hurt is not one of the tests. If someone has seriously hurt you, you may never forget it. However, many times I have been offended or hurt by someone and quickly forgave them. Weeks later I remember something happened but I don't remember the details. I have actually forgotten the incident. That's a great blessing but not a test of forgiveness. When we stop harboring the bitterness of an offense it will gradually move out of our conscience thoughts.

WHAT'S NEXT?

There are three parts to the forgiveness process. Giving forgiveness, when you have been hurt, seeking forgiveness when you have hurt another, and reconciling and restoring the relationship once the offenses have been forgiven. You have seen how to give forgiveness, which may be the most difficult part. But what if you have hurt someone else? How can you seek their forgiveness and then work with them to reconcile and restore your relationship? You will find the answers in the next few chapters!

Appendix A

Four lists to prepare to forgive someone.

List this person's name _____

1. What did this person do or not do to hurt you? This would include such things as: embarrass you, cheat you, deceive you, trick you, slander you, betray you, or abuse you verbally, sexually, physically or mentally. Be as specific as you need to be.

_____

_____

_____

_____

_____

_____

_____

2. Now make a list of how you felt. This would include such feelings as: defiled, hustled, cheated, ridiculed, used, unworthy, scorned, taken advantage of, taken for granted, unappreciated, confused, shocked, or rejected.

_____

_____

_____

_____

_____

_____

_____

3. Your next list is the ramifications of the hurt. What the person did is like a rock hitting the pond. The ramifications are the ongoing hurts or ripples extending from the initial impact. As you make up this list consider all seven areas of life: physically, spiritually, psychologically, financially, martially, parentally, and socially. All will not apply but several will.

_____

_____

_____

_____

_____

_____

4. Finally list your sinful reactions. These could include: bitterness, resentment, slander, gossip, verbal attacks, desire for revenge, anger, silence or other ways to punish such as snubbing or back stabbing, and sarcasm.

_____

_____

_____

_____

_____

_____

I AM THE OFFENDED

1

GUILTY! I sentence you...

OFFENDER

JUDGE

OFFENDED

OFFENDED

When I am offended, in my mind I see the offender as guilty. Only God has the right to execute judgment (Ps. 9:7-8; Acts 17:31). My attempt to lay guilt on the offender by setting a standard is reacting after the flesh. For example: "This person should not have treated me that way" (Matthew 7:1-5).

200-E

THE RESULTS OF MY FLESHLY REACTIONS

2

I may react silently and "stuff" my bitterness or wrath. Or I may express it in abusive speech or actions, slander, or swearing. The result is the same.

Ephesians 4:26-27, 31-32
1 Peter 5:8-9
Ecclesiastes 7:9

Going to bed angry gives the Devil a foothold to torment me, a child of God. I am actually held prisoner by reacting after the flesh. This control of the flesh and torment by the Devil can only be stopped by extending forgiveness. The offender should ask forgiveness from me, but may never do so. Consequently, I must initiate forgiveness. Notice I have the keys to freedom in my hand.

anger

rage

spite

ramifications

bitterness

slander

quarreling

silence

200-E1

I CHOOSE TO EXTEND FORGIVENESS

3

I can achieve freedom by extending forgiveness. By using these keys I am set free from the prison and torment. Now the truth about me can be seen and realized.

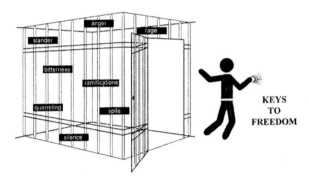

KEYS
TO
FREEDOM

Key #1 -   I admit to God how I felt regarding this offense (Psalm 62:8).

Key #2 -   I admit to God that I have been holding the person guilty for the act, the hurt, and the ramifications of the offense (Luke 6:37; Rom. 2:1).

Key #3 -   I now extend (give freely) my forgiveness to the person for that action, my hurt, and the ramifications of the action. This forgiveness is extending grace to the offender as Christ extended grace to me (Eph. 4:32; Col. 3:13).

Key #4 -   I now put the offender into God's hands and let go. I will allow God to work in this person's life in His time (1 Peter 5:7).

Key #5 -   I now name and confess (agree with God) that my sinful reactions and attitudes (including holding the offender guilty) were wrong. I ask God to show me areas of godship and repent (1 John 1:9).

Key #6 -   I choose to live as the new creation that I am (2 Cor. 5:17). This means I accept that God has forgiven me, and I lay aside my fleshly reactions (Eph. 4:31; Col. 3:8, 12).

Key #7 -   I tell God I am willing to be reconciled to the offender and allow Him to love the offender through me (2 Cor. 5:18; Col. 3:14; Heb. 12:14).

200-E2

VCL
VICTORIOUS CHRISTIAN LIVING Conference
Copyright © 1998 Victorious Christian Living International, Inc.

The Freedom to Love and Live Again

Chapter Nine

How to Seek True Forgiveness

(Story told by LuAnn, Sharon and Ray)

Well, did you do it? Did you take the time to actually forgive someone after reading the last chapter? If you did, then you are ready for the next step.

This is a transcript of an actual radio conversation between a US Naval ship and Canadian authorities off the coast of Newfoundland, in October of 1995. It was retrieved off the Internet.

> *U.S. SHIP: Please divert your course 0.5 degrees to the South to avoid a collision.*
>
> *CANADIAN REPLY: Recommend you divert YOUR course 15 degrees to the South to avoid a collision.*
>
> *U.S. SHIP: This is the Captain of the US Navy Ship. I say again, divert YOUR course.*
>
> *CANADIAN REPLY: No, I say again, divert YOUR course!*
>
> *U.S. SHIP: This is the aircraft Carrier USS Missouri. We are a LARGE warship of the US NAVY. DIVERT YOUR COURSE NOW*
>
> *CANADIAN REPLY: This is a lighthouse. Your call.*

Do you think that the Captain of the Navy ship quickly sent back this message: "I'm sorry, I didn't realize you were a lighthouse, would you please forgive me, I was wrong." I don't think so.

All of a sudden, people are shooting each other on the freeways. Why? What's behind this new phenomenon, "Road Rage"? One reason is that people are offended and no one is willing to seek forgiveness.

We had an incident in Phoenix recently that demonstrates this point. A driver cut off another man in traffic. Feeling angry, the motorist who had been cut-off followed the other man to his destination—his job. He yelled at the man and swore at him for not

83

being a more courteous driver. And what did the offender do? Did he yell back, "Hey, man, I'm sorry, I was wrong for cutting you off. My head was not in my driving, would you please forgive me?" No, he started yelling and swearing right back, defending himself.

So, the driver who had been cut off pulled out a gun and shot the other man in the chest.

You've seen the power of forgiveness at work in the course of this book. But perhaps you don't feel it incumbent upon you to go and seek the forgiveness of those you have hurt or offended: "If forgiving is so great, then they can go ahead and forgive me. They don't need me to come crawling over on my hands and knees."

Let's take a look at how some of the people you've met previously sought forgiveness. In Chapter Five you read Rocky and LuAnn's story. Listen to LuAnn tell us about that crucial moment when she found out what she had to forgive:

At dinner one night, Rocky took my hands as his eyes filled with tears and said, "Lu, I've been unfaithful." I was in a state of shock and could hardly comprehend what I had been told. My stomach shut down and seemed to send a message to my heart: closed indefinitely ... [But] for the first time in our marriage I had my husband. He was no longer loyal to himself or another woman. He cared only to be obedient to God and loyal to me. In a time of great pain, I felt the sweetness of Rocky's love for me, as I had never known it before.

Also, God was speaking to me and showing me that I was not an innocent party. He had convicted me before Rocky's confession that I had isolated myself from him and had not been the wife God had designed and commanded me to be. I confessed to Rocky that I had not given myself to him mentally, emotionally, or spiritually and I asked for his forgiveness. Rocky said something I'll never forget. "You never needed me, and a man needs to be needed." He gave me his forgiveness and more - an understanding of his need.

This heart-warming account shows the value of seeking forgiveness. Rocky sought LuAnn's forgiveness and opened the door for <u>her</u> to seek <u>his</u> forgiveness as well. When two people are sensitive to the work of God in their lives, this synchronization will often occur.

Recently I was counseling a teenage boy who was having troubles in his Christian high school. As we talked we realized that his main problem was not school at all, but his teacher. She was always "on his case" about his hair, his earrings, his choice of clothes, and his general attitude in class. Instead of trying to defend the teacher I went through the process of forgiveness, explained in the last chapter.

The teen filled out his four lists. He wrote that his teacher had offended him (the act), embarrassed him (his feelings), and that he felt her attitude was affecting his grades (ramifications). He prayed and forgave her. When he finished he looked up and said, "Wow, now I see how rude I have been toward her. Man, I need to go and seek her forgiveness."

I was shocked. This young man was convicted of his sinful reactions <u>while</u> forgiving another person and was ready to seek forgiveness. He listed his sinful reactions as: not looking at her when she spoke to him, speaking disrespectfully, and even walking away when she was talking to him. He went and asked for her forgiveness.

WHY DO WE NEED TO SEEK FORGIVENESS?

Many Christians face disasters in their lives because they need to seek someone's forgiveness but don't do it. Jesus was concerned about how we treat each other and prayed about it in John 17. Listen to His heart: *My prayer is not for them alone. I pray also for those who will believe in me through their message, (that's you and me) that all of them may be <u>one</u>, Father, just as you are in me and I am in you. May they also be in us so that the world may believe that you have sent me. I have given them the glory that you gave me, that they may be <u>one</u> as we are one: I in them and you in me. May they be brought to complete <u>unity</u> to let the world know that you sent me and have loved them even as you have loved Me.* (John 17:20-23 NIV; emphasis added)

Jesus yearns and prays for our unity and oneness. We can maintain that unity and harmony by being quick to seek forgiveness when we offend our brethren. Why should you seek forgiveness? Because Jesus desires oneness in the body of Christ.

John's first epistle holds a key insight into seeking forgiveness. *But if we walk in the light as He Himself is in the light, we have fellowship with one another, and the blood of Jesus His Son cleanses us from all sin.* (1 John 1:1) The Living Bible makes this even clearer: *But if we are living in the light of God's presence, just as Christ does, then we have **wonderful fellowship and joy with each other**, and the blood of Jesus His Son cleanses us from every sin* (emphasis added). Walking in the light is not hiding. It is admitting when we have hurt another person and quickly seeking forgiveness. When you know that you have offended another person and you walk away, you are walking in darkness.

I'm sure you've felt that tug at your heart to go and seek forgiveness from someone, but you said to yourself, "Oh, I'm sure it wasn't that big a deal, I'm not going to do it." That could be the first step of your walk in darkness. Even the simple act of avoiding a person because you feel guilty being around them is a way to walk in darkness. When in doubt, err on the side of seeking forgiveness too much, rather than not at all.

Consider the bad example of King David and his relationship with Bathsheba. David committed adultery with Uriah's wife. And once he had done so, he walked in darkness and hid his sin. Let's revisit this fascinating story from 2 Samuel 11.

After Uriah returned from battle David talked with him. David tried to get Uriah to go to his house and sleep with Bathsheba, but Uriah wouldn't do it. He was such a loyal man to David and said, *The ark and Israel and Judah are staying in temporary shelters, and my lord Joab and the servants of my lord are camping in the open field. Shall I then go to my house to eat and to drink and to lie with my wife? By your life and the life of your soul, I will not do this thing.* (2 Samuel 11:11)

So David got him drunk, but still Uriah refused to go home. Now David was desperate. He planned a way for Uriah to be killed in battle and wrote a note to Joab who was David's chief military leader. His cunning and deceit is reminiscent of a modern day "hit man" hired to kill someone and told that their death must look "accidental".

David knew that no one would find anything strange about a military man being killed in a battle. This was a vicious plot to walk in darkness. And what harvest did David reap from his sins? His child, conceived in adultery with Bathsheba, died.

Think how differently things could have turned out if David had spoken truthfully to Uriah and sought his forgiveness, saying, "Uriah, my friend and warrior, while you were risking your life to protect me, I have done a terrible thing. I have slept with your wife. I was so wrong. Could you please find it in your heart to forgive me? She is your wife and I will see to it that the child is cared for and I will make it up to you in any way you see fit." And David would be walking in the light! Of course, it would have been difficult, but consider the consequences of the alternative: an innocent soldier and an innocent child, dead.

So, why seek forgiveness? To walk in the light.

Sharon, in Chapter Six, walked in the light with her boss:

One of the most exciting times of seeking forgiveness was when I went to my former employer to confess stealing all that money - $10,000. I took a good friend with me because I knew I might go to jail. I asked for forgiveness from my boss for stealing and he said yes. Then I asked if he would forgive or cancel my debt. By the grace of God, he did. That was such a freedom. All the weight of that sin was gone. As I continued to ask forgiveness for past offenses, more relief came to my life. Now I am current in asking for forgiveness as the Holy Spirit leads me to. I lay myself, my pride, down and ask them to forgive me. No excuses, just, "I was wrong. Will you forgive me?" My friends and family continue to love me.

Sharon has shown us the way God works on our behalf when we are obedient to seek forgiveness. Her boss not only forgave her, but also released her from paying the debt. We cannot always predict the outcome, in some cases a person may go to jail. But we still must do what God says.

Notice Sharon's simple way of seeking forgiveness. She says seven little words: "I was wrong. Will you forgive me?" That's how simple it can be.

WHEN DO WE NEED TO SEEK FORGIVENESS?

If therefore you are presenting your offering at the altar, and there remember that your brother has something against you, leave your offering there before the altar, and go your way; first be reconciled to your brother, and then come and present your offering. (Matthew 5:23-24)

The first word in verse twenty-four is "leave." That word is in the active imperative tense in the Greek. It is a command. The words, "go your way" are also in the same active imperative tense. This is serious. If you are even getting ready to give a gift to God and remember someone from whom you need to seek forgiveness then you are to <u>stop</u> what you are doing and <u>go</u> seek forgiveness. When is this to happen? <u>Right Now.</u>

The moment that you feel the impression of the Holy Spirit, reminding you to seek forgiveness, <u>that</u> is the time to do it. How interesting it would be if, in our churches on Sunday, just prior to receiving the morning offering, the Pastor would say, "Now before we receive the offering I want you to take a moment to make sure no one is holding anything against you. Go to your brothers and sisters right now and seek forgiveness if you need to. Also, we have installed several phones for your use, at no cost, to call friends and relatives." Wouldn't that be wild? It might seem strange, but this is exactly what Jesus was teaching His men. If such an announcement were made each week it would serve as a gentle reminder of the need to maintain relationships and pursue reconciliation.

Jesus commands us to seek forgiveness right away, without delay.

HOW DO WE PREPARE TO SEEK FORGIVENESS?

1. Before you talk to the person you have offended, you must first talk to God.

    King David understood this when he repented and said, *Against you, you only, have I sinned and done what is evil in your sight, so that you are proved right when you speak and justified when you judge.* (Psalm 51:4 NIV) He saw that a sin against another person was also a sin against God. What he did was evil in God's sight. When we hurt someone, we have done evil in God's sight. So we must begin by asking God for his forgiveness. In this, as in all life, God comes first. Paul tells us, *In view of this, I also do my best to maintain always a blameless conscience both before God and before men.* (Acts 24:16)

88

The vertical precedes the horizontal.

First admit to God that your action or words hurt another person. What you did violated Christ's words: *A new command I give you: Love one another. As I have loved you, so you must love one another. By this all men will know that you are my disciples, if you love one another.* (John 13:34-35 NIV)

Tell God: "Lord, this was not a loving word or action toward _____ (the person you offended). Thank You for convicting me of this wrong. I repent and receive Your forgiveness right now." You could also thank the Lord Jesus for dying for that sin and making forgiveness toward you possible. God is the initiator of forgiveness. He made it possible for you to be united to Him. Now He wants you to be united to others.

2. Prior to seeking forgiveness from someone you must first forgive that person. This is important. If you don't forgive you will tend to place blame or accuse the person. Your attempt to seek forgiveness could sound like this, "I would like you to forgive me blowing up and saying hurtful things to you. But I was just responding to your attacks upon me. You were so rude that night I felt attacked and leveled by your insensitive comments. I was wrong but so were you." If you haven't forgiven the other person, you could quickly find yourself immersed in self-justification. As you approach the person you must not see that person as guilty. If you have forgiven them as outlined in the last chapter, they will not be guilty in your eyes.

3. As you consider talking to the person you hurt, you need to think about what you will say. Review the offense clearly. You may need to have a pastor or counselor to help you to see how you offended the other person. Have them help you to see how deeply you may have hurt the one you offended. They might ask you questions to draw out all the details of the hurtful incident. What did you say? What was your attitude? How long have you treated that person in that manner? How would you feel if someone had treated you in this way? Review all these questions and write out some

of the things that you will say when you go to seek forgiveness.

4. Evaluate what seeking forgiveness is <u>not</u>. It is not "apologizing" or "being sorry" for what you did. Those are not sinful words but they are weak. It is also not trying to make up for what you did by being nice. It's not trying to buy someone with acts of kindness.

5. Good timing is vital. When is the right time to seek forgiveness? When you are both able to talk undisturbed for several minutes. You could even say, "Is this a good time to talk? I have something important to discuss." If the person says, "No" then set a time when you are both free. Don't seek forgiveness from your wife when the TV is on, the kids are crying, and the kitchen is a mess.

6. Sometimes I hear, "I want to talk to this person but they won't talk to me. I know I've really hurt them. What do I do?" Try calling on the phone. If they don't hang up on you, say quickly, "Hi, this is_____ . I really want to talk to you to tell you how very wrong I have been." People we have hurt love to hear us crawl. Actually it is the Lord producing His humility in us. Sometimes I have suggested people go to the home of the one they hurt and talk. One lady wouldn't even open the screen door but she did listen to the offender explain how wrong she had been. They were reconciled.

HOW DO WE SEEK TRUE FORGIVENESS?

Now you are ready to go to the person you have offended to seek forgiveness. Ask the Lord to give you a gentle and humble heart. Remember, it is often not <u>what</u> you say but <u>how</u> you say it.

1. Don't drag it out. Only go into as much detail as necessary. This is not a time to defend yourself or explain why you did what you did. If you spend too much time warming up, you will weaken the process. If you are seeking forgiveness from a teenager it should only last about 47 seconds. If you go on and on their eyes will glaze over and they will think, "Oh no, another lecture."

2. Go in person. That's the best way.

3. There are two exceptions to this. First, if you were involved in an immoral relationship <u>don't</u> go in person. One man said, "Tonight, I'll go over to her house and tell her the affair is over." NO! We made a phone call and I listened as he stopped the affair.

4. Second, a telephone is a good way to seek forgiveness if you simply can't go in person, such as when people live hundreds or thousands of miles away.

5. Say the three hardest words in the English language: I WAS WRONG. Saying you were wrong is much stronger than saying you were sorry. You are taking responsibility for your actions. Do not let your pride stand in the way of saying those words. Remember the TV series, "Happy Days?" In one episode, Fonzie had to learn how to say he was wrong. He, the epitome of pride, couldn't do it. Those three words stuck in his throat like a dry piece of bread wrapped around peanut butter. God is the only One who can give you victory over your pride. Your entire statement could sound like this, "I was wrong regarding (what you did or said). Would you please forgive me?" That's it!

6. Don't write a letter. I am amazed at how many people tell me, "Yea, I feel really badly about what happened, I'm going to write a letter and seek forgiveness." NO! NO! NO! There are several reasons why that's not a good idea. First, with E-mail, fax machines, copy machines and the Internet, your letter could be sent around the world in minutes. Do you want that to happen? Think about who might be reading it tomorrow.

   Second, a letter can be misunderstood. It is very hard to express feelings and tone of voice in a letter. Finally, there is no sense of closure from a letter. You could wait for months for an answer and not receive one.

   If you feel strongly that you must write out your feelings, try this: Write the letter. Put all your thoughts in it. Then go to the person and read the letter aloud. Or call them on the phone if you can't get to them in person.

* * *

Now, finally, let's look at a story you haven't heard before. Ray, who spent much of his life as a traveling salesman and is now a minister, tells us about seeking his daughter's forgiveness for something "trivial," and the effect it had on her:

Ephesians 6:4 says, **And you, fathers do not provoke your children to wrath, but bring them up in the training of the Lord.** *I read this, of course but never thought about it in conjunction with my own fathering skills. I wasn't a father, anyway. I was a dictator.*

I thought that children must jump when you told them to, and I gave them no slack. In fact, I felt that if I asked or demanded something of my children, no matter if it was humiliating or even inconsequential, they were going to do it. That was just the way it was.

As I attended VCL training, my heart began to soften and my eyes were opened to my failings as a father and a husband. Through counseling I was shown that I must reconcile with my family. I began reconciliation with a list of offenses that I had committed against my four daughters. I met with them individually to share my heart and to ask them for their forgiveness.

My eldest daughter sat in my bedroom and I began with an item so trivial that I almost hadn't listed it. But I believed that God had given me the list, so I went ahead. I reminded her of the time I had asked her to sing, in front of her sisters, a silly song about a gazebo. She had refused so then I told her to sing. She still hadn't wanted to, so I required her to sing. It was a song that made fun of her, which made her the object of ridicule and laughter. I had humiliated her, so I asked her to forgive me.

As I told the story, she began to cry! She told me that this incident had always bothered her, and was one of the reasons she did not want to go into counseling, though she eventually did. She told her counselor that what I had done to her simply wasn't fair. The counselor told her that in order to make progress she would have to forgive her father. She did and was set free.

By asking for her forgiveness, I had taken away the sting that the "gazebo incident" caused in her life. I have often reflected on that. I could hardly have imagined the impact so small an action could have on a young life.

My wife and daughters have forgiven me for my transgressions and, for the first time, I have begun to truly enjoy the happiness of being a father and a husband. My family and I can walk in the Scripture of Ephesians 4:31-32: **Let all bitterness and wrath and anger and clamor and slander be put away from you, along with all malice. And be kind to one another, tender-hearted, forgiving each other, just as God in Christ also has forgiven you.**

I promise you from the bottom of my heart that there is real joy in getting forgiveness. God joins you as you obey Him. This should be a way of life. Just as soon as you are aware by the work of the Holy Spirit that you have hurt someone you need to go and ask them for their forgiveness.

Have you been like the Naval Captain at the beginning of this chapter? Have you been running into lighthouses? Have you left people emotionally shipwrecked? Now (not next week) is the time to humble yourself and go ask for forgiveness.

Who has God brought to your mind? Make a list.

_____

_____

_____

_____

_____

_____

Now, trust God and prepare to meet with the first one. God will give you what you need as you depend on Him. Let these words from 1 Peter 5:5-6 encourage you: *God opposes the proud but gives grace to the humble. Humble yourselves, therefore, under God's mighty hand, that he may lift you up in due time.* (NIV)

The Freedom to Love and Live Again

Chapter Ten

The Crown Jewel of Forgiveness

(Story told by Mark)

Jesus is waiting to make your life new. Do you long to have the kind of relationships with others that Christ makes possible? Have you begun the journey, in search of true freedom to love and live again? Are you beginning to understand the depth of God's love and forgiveness of you? If so, perhaps you have been prompted to give forgiveness to someone you have resented because of an offense against you. Maybe you have even been convicted to seek forgiveness from someone and have acted on that conviction. Now you are nearing the end of the journey.

Don't stop yet. You are about to discover the crown jewel of forgiveness: rebuilding relationships. Few make it this far down the road, and those who don't are missing out on the most satisfying part of forgiveness. Even fewer follow through to the end and actually experience the fullness of the life of Christ.

Obviously, giving and seeking forgiveness is only a part of the process, not the whole. But exactly how do we go about rebuilding relationships that are damaged? In order to experience God's healing, we must understand His process and commit to follow His direction.

Some do not experience immediate relief when forgiveness has been given. But if you are obedient to God, He promises to remove the pain as soon as His will is fulfilled. *For thus says the high and exalted One Who lives forever, whose name is Holy, "I dwell on a high and holy place, And also with the contrite and lowly of spirit in order to revive the spirit of the lowly and to revive the heart of the contrite. For I will not contend forever, neither will I always be angry; For the spirit would grow faint before Me, and the breath of those whom I have made. Because of the iniquity of his unjust gain I was angry and struck him; I hid My face and was angry, and* he went on turning away, in the way of his heart. I have seen his ways, but I will heal him; I will lead him and restore comfort to him and to his mourners, creating the praise of the lips. Peace, peace to him who is far and to him who is near," says the Lord, "and I will heal him" (Isaiah 57:15-19).

There is an end to the pain, but it will only occur when both the offender and the offended realize that God has a message of life for both of you. God uses conflict in relationships to get our attention, so that He can change the lives of everyone involved.

The Lord used conflict in Mark and Sue's family to get their attention. Here is how Mark describes their conflict:

I caused Sue serious damage out of my selfishness. It seemed harmless to me, but the ramifications of my choices were far more complex than I ever imagined. I wanted to be a good missionary, but I became bitter toward my wife because she kept threatening to go back to the United States. To silence her threats, in a heated argument, I told her that if she did not stop trying to derail the Lord's work in Papua New Guinea, the Lord was going to grant her wish by taking my life. "You will go back to the United States a widow," I said.

All I wanted was for her to stop threatening to go home so I could do my work. I didn't know all the damage my foolish statement would cause. She stopped her threats, but I didn't win. In fact, I had blasphemed God's holy character before the woman I was supposed to be leading in righteousness. Basically, I told her that if she didn't do what I wanted, God would kill me. I painted a picture of the Holy One as a supreme terrorist. Why would she trust, love, and worship Him?

I didn't realize that my wife's heart had been deeply wounded by several authorities in her life. Her father had abandoned her as a child. "Authorities are untrustworthy," she concluded. Though she and her stepfather are now reconciled, there were some serious offenses between them as well. Thus, another opportunity to view authorities as untrustworthy. I had married her to take her out of all her misery, but on the mission field I completed the picture that "authorities are untrustworthy."

The finished product of my selfishness was a woman who despised all authority and would not trust it in any form. What was worse, she would not trust God. After all, He was just another authority who uses people for His own purposes. "How can anyone live without trusting God," I wondered. But I had never considered all the ramifications of my selfish sin when I unknowingly labeled God the supreme terrorist.

It is important for Mark and Sue to look at hardship with expectation, because God is in charge and is doing a work in both of their lives, every minute of their lives. They must learn what Lisa learned: that God is totally sovereign, and He loves us enough to use even the very difficult circumstances in our lives to enable us to live the supernatural life of Jesus Christ. Both have the opportunity to know a deeper relationship with the Father. They can grow in gratitude to God for their new life, and they are left with absolutely no reason for separation in their relationship to one another.

There are at least two parties in every broken relationship: the offender and the offended. Chances are, each person fits each category to varying degrees. We will discuss the process of rebuilding relationships from both perspectives.

Whether you are the offender or the offended, you must realize that the restoration process <u>is not about you</u>. If you are the offender, Satan will tell you otherwise. He quietly whispers: "Boy, <u>you</u> blew it this time. <u>You</u> are worthless. <u>You</u> are a failure. Why don't you just give up?" You may feel defeated, as though there is no way to recover from your sin. You may believe that things will never change. But there is hope when you follow the path of forgiveness.

If you are the offended, the Lord also desires you to be molded into the image of Christ. It may be hard to accept that, especially in the midst of pain. But quiet your heart before the Lord and let Him speak to you from His heart.

As the offender, there is a need to understand why you sinned. You sinned because you decided that there was a need in your life and you attempted to fill that need with something that went directly against God's will. Mark determined that his need was to be a good missionary and he hurt his wife trying to make it happen. Did Mark satisfy his need? Did he come out ahead? No. In fact, there were some pretty serious losses.

So, what do you do with your thoughts about this need that you think you have? You must realize that only God has the right to determine your needs. If you determine them, you are playing god. Mark thought he needed to do whatever it took to be a good missionary.

Here is how the Bible says you are to live: *As you therefore have received Christ Jesus the Lord, so walk in Him, having been firmly rooted and now being built up in Him and established in your faith, just as you were instructed, and overflowing with gratitude* (Colossians 2:6-7). Your life in Christ began in faith, and this is how you must live right now. Not by sight. You have all you need if you have Him. God knows your needs and guarantees to meet them. Depend on the Lord instead of your own faulty perceptions.

* * *

Reconciliation of relationships is God's idea. He designed it and He desires it. Mark and Sue were faithful to pursue reconciliation, and the Lord blessed them:

The Lord brought us home from the mission field, but my value as a missionary was lost. I shifted my crumbling value from "missionary" to "pastor." I eventually ended up at VCL International a broken man. I went because my daughter, Tricia, had experienced some very serious emotional trauma. This was the first time in my life I had met a situation I couldn't control. But things had not yet come to a head. The damage I caused my wife was being passed on to my kids.

I began the discipleship process at VCLI and wanted to finish training so I could be a better pastor at my church. During the third level of training, my trainer challenged me by revealing some of the smoldering coals of unforgiveness that were stuffed down inside. I kept my standards to myself so I would not hurt my "mission-field-battered" wife any deeper. I asked Sue if she sensed any standard I had placed on her and her response devastated me. "Mark, I have <u>never</u> thought I could be the wife I know you want. I have always thought of myself as a disappointment to you."

That night we began to allow the Lord to work out this miracle of forgiveness. It was a wonderful beginning step, but I had yet to enter God's refining fire. God wanted to do a work in my family.

The Crown Jewel of Forgiveness

One day, while pulling into the parking lot of our ministry, I discovered the remains of a marijuana cigarette on the dashboard of my pickup. I also found a sandwich bag with marijuana in it. It was my daughter's. I was numb.

I also had a run in with one of my sons who loved to party. While I was trying to sell our home, Brian was getting drunk with his friends and leaving bottles and cans strewn all over the yard. After a few pleas and a final warning, I told Brian to leave the house. I was defeated. Two of my four children had gotten into all the sin they could find, and Pastor Mark was finished. I was ready to leave the ministry. My children had felt abandoned, just like my wife, while I did what made me feel valued.

I had failed as a father, husband, pastor, and missionary. All the things I tried to do to be valued as a man in ministry failed. I learned wonderful truth through my training at VCLI, but the Lord was giving me the chance to live what I had learned. I learned to trust God.

I went to my daughter and told her I found the marijuana, but of course, she said it wasn't hers. I told her it didn't matter any more, that our game was going to change. After years of trying shear force and discipline to get my children to walk in step with me, I lost the war. I couldn't control my daughter.

I sought her forgiveness for trying to manipulate her by what she called "the look," and by being unreasonable in correction and threats. She was caught red-handed, so hearing her father ask her for forgiveness was a shock to her. "Sure, Dad, I forgive you," she said.

She had shown me she would not live under my direction or protection, so I gave up all rules and curfews. "You have freedom as an adult, and all the responsibilities. That means if you come home pregnant, you are on your own." I also told her I would not be responsible for any consequences she might incur using drugs, or for other poor choices.

"I love you," I said, "and it is my fault that I have had to make this hard adjustment. But that is the way it will be. Will you forgive me for failing you so miserably?" It was a shock to her, and she certainly wasn't expecting that. But she told me later that my action caused her to see reality.

Brian was a different story. He was already on his own. I asked him to forgive me for some of the same sins I confessed to Tricia. I told him I loved him and it was ripping my heart out to see the chances he was taking with his life. I asked him to forgive me for hounding him and "beating him" with my Bible. It seemed like we experienced forgiveness right away. The stab in the heart came when I realized that Brian was not yet done with his course, even though he had forgiven me. I gave up my rights to keep my son and God put Brian through the wringer.

He burned up the engine in his car and I helped him replace it. But it was stolen three times and finally stripped and burned to a crisp. He was down, but not yet defeated. I continued giving up my right to lead him as a father, and I trusted the Lord to change him. Then the Lord began taking away his friends. One went to prison and the other walked out of his life because of a fight over a woman. Now there was nothing left.

Brian eventually came around and I reconciled with my children. At the time of this writing, both Tricia and Brian are in training at VCL International. Brian is currently completing the third level of training, and Tricia will begin the third level in a few months. She plans to be in full-time service for the Lord.

My God reigns! I did nothing to cause the healing that has taken place in the lives of my kids. I just took my hands off and allowed the Lord to do the work He promised to do.

The icing on the cake is that my wife, Sue, now works with me at VCL International, in the accounting department. I serve with her every day. God has healed my life with Him, with my wife, with my kids, and with my ministry. Through all I suffered, I learned that my ministry is not my life, my relationship with the Lord is. My value comes from who I am in Christ, not who I am in ministry.

Healing took place in Mark's family. Let's look at some aspects of God's healing process:

1. Checking heart attitudes.
2. Understanding the damage that was done.
3. Assessing God's resources for healing. (His promises and my responsibilities.)
4. Beginning the healing.

CHECKING THE HEART ATTITUDE
Repentance

The first step of healing for the offender and the offended is repentance.

That may seem unreasonable if you are the offended person. After all, you are the abused, damaged party, just like Sue. But what the Lord wants to reveal to you has nothing to do with what the offender did to you. Instead, consider how the offense affected you. Consider what happened after the shock settled.

When Lisa was raped, she did not want to have anything to do with the offender. What she revealed was that she never wanted to be vulnerable to being hurt again, so she took her trust out of the Lord's hands and put her confidence in herself. She exercised godship by trying to control all of life and avoid any chance of pain. She also established a standard that she expected God to live by: life should be pain-free and comfortable. Jesus is the model we are to follow. Where would we be if Jesus had valued comfort over obedience?

If you have been offended, perhaps the Lord wants to set you free from the lie that you cannot be happy unless your conditions are met. God will likely call you to repent of your godship, just as He called LuAnn to repent of seeking to have her needs met apart from God.

If you are the offender, the Lord is definitely calling you to repent of your wrong attitudes and actions toward the offended person. Mark was called to repent of his attitudes and actions that hurt Sue.

Repentance begins with honest appraisal. You must "get real" with the Lord. But don't focus on repenting of single choices. Repent of self-reliant, self-focused, independent attitudes and habits that are not in agreement with the Lord.

These are important questions for offenders and those who have been offended: Have you lived, thinking that your life is your own? Are you ready to repent of taking control of aspects of your life where your purposes oppose God? Can you face a situation and say, as Jesus did, "Father, not my will, but yours be done"? It is essential before you can begin to reconcile a broken relationship.

Blame

The offended person will often play the "blame game." It doesn't work any better today than it did in the Garden of Eden. As you focus on blame, and on what you have lost as a consequence of someone else's sin, you are likely to become focused on yourself. Self-focus leads to godship—wanting what you want, when you want it. Don't forfeit your joy by focusing on your losses, or by allowing your feelings to dictate your actions or attitudes. Keep your thoughts and feelings before the Lord.

Offenders often see themselves as victims, even though they did the damage. "I wouldn't have done that if you hadn't..." A "victim mentality" keeps you from repenting. Take responsibility for your own attitudes and actions, apart from the attitudes and actions of anyone else. No one can <u>make</u> you do anything.

Self-focus

Correct focus will be on restoring a right relationship with God through repentance, then rebuilding right relationships with others through forgiveness. There is no self-focus in God's scheme of things. Continuing to measure life using self as the standard will only make things worse.

Philippians 2:3 says, *Do nothing from selfishness or empty conceit, but with humility of mind let each of you regard one another as more important than himself.* People who live according to that verse have lives filled with quality relationships and the Lord's blessing.

UNDERSTANDING THE DAMAGE THAT WAS DONE

In our counseling offices, we often hear offenders say, "I had no idea how much damage my choice would cause." Mark had no idea of the damage done to Sue, Brian, and Tricia. The total devastation cannot be calculated prior to the sin. Part of God's healing process in the lives of the offender and the offended is to understand the damage. When the offender begins to understand the damage done to the offended person it shows the offended person that the offender values them.

Rocky and LuAnn talked about their feelings often during the time of damage assessment. Their willingness to confront these difficult emotions resulted in swifter healing and reconciliation of the relationship.

As the offended person, you may be inclined to "blow off" your losses and get on with life. In our ministry, we often deal with people whose lives are crippled because of long-standing hurts. Some have forgiven the offender for their actions, but have not forgiven them for all the ramification of the offense. If you don't want to face your feelings, you will be hiding away a smoldering coal that will continue to burn inside of you. It may seem more comfortable not to talk about your feelings, it only hinders the healing process.

ASSESSING THE RESOURCES FOR HEALING
The Promises

Resources for healing are infinite for the offender and the offended.

Colossians 1:9-13 offers some promises. Let's examine those verses. *For this reason also, since the day we heard of it, we have not ceased to pray for you and to ask that you may be filled with the knowledge of His will in all spiritual wisdom and understanding* (verse 9). You are filled with the knowledge of His will! What stands in contrast to that? Your will! That is why it is important to give up your selfish desires, like being valued for what you do.

So that you may walk in a manner worthy of the Lord, to please Him in all respects, bearing fruit in every good work and increasing in the knowledge of God (verse 10). When you walk in a manner worthy of the Lord He will keep you living in the center of what He wants for you, attaining His blessings and pleasing Him in all aspects. You will also increase in the knowledge of God.

Strengthened with all power, according to His glorious might, for the attaining of all steadfastness and patience (verse 11). Would you like to be strengthened with all power? That's His promise when we walk in obedience!

Joyously giving thanks to the Father, who has qualified us to share in the inheritance of the saints in light (verse 12). If you have forgotten what it means to share in the inheritance, go back and read Lisa's testimony! The inheritance is the deep, rich, powerful, dynamic life of Christ. It is yours to enjoy when you are obedient to the things of the Lord.

For He delivered us from the domain of darkness, and transferred us to the kingdom of His beloved Son (verse 13). He has transferred you out of death into light! It is the work of Christ alone. You don't have to sin any more.

God's Word is jam-packed with promises of God, and in Christ, they are already fulfilled! That is what makes forgiveness possible. Mark now experiences a living reality that Christ is life. He doesn't need to worry about the trouble his kids are in. He trusts the almighty God of the universe. Why? Because His promises are not only true, they are fulfilled through faith.

Cling to the promise of God, no matter what you see on the horizon. As you cling to the promises of God and follow the Lord through restoration and healing, you please God and attain the victor's crown through your faith and trust in Jesus Christ.

My Responsibilities

You might not see your responsibilities as resources for rebuilding your relationship, but they are. By taking responsibility, you regain what you forfeited through your sin. Here are some responsibilities of both the offender and the offended:

- Accountability. Often people say, "I want you to hold me accountable." That is a fallacy. You have the responsibility to <u>make</u> yourself accountable to others. They are not responsible, you are. Faithfulness needs to be demonstrated to earn trust.

- Walk in the light. God loves light, so don't give your sin darkness to hide in. *He who conceals his transgressions will not prosper, but he who confesses and forsakes them will find compassion* (Proverbs 28:13). Don't give your flesh a breeding ground.

- Rebuilding trust. Trust is the unquestioned belief in integrity, strength, or ability. All relationships require trust. If you break trust in a relationship, you must earn it back. Without demanding, or even expecting, another person to do anything differently, accept your responsibility in every way, accept what is happening, and don't try to escape the consequences of whatever happened to break trust. When the track record is established, trust can be rebuilt.

- Forgive, and let God cause you to forget. "I can forgive, but I can't forget." God empowers you to forgive. As you trust God, He will cause you to forget your pain.
- Forgive, even if the offender is not repentant. God's will for you is forgiveness, whether the offender repents or not.
- Be responsible for your choices. Don't clutter things up by including the offender or his actions when the Lord is dealing with you and your actions. It would be easy for any of the people in this book to let the actions of another hinder their obedience to God. But they didn't, and that is why they live in freedom today! Take responsibility so that His purifying work will build character and strength in you. God wants to make you His beloved, totally dependent servant. Don't let someone else or their actions stand in the way.
- Forgive as often as it takes. How often do you have to forgive? Only as often as you want to be blessed. There is always the possibility that the offender will fall again. Prepare yourself to trust the Lord, no matter what.
- Deny yourself your "rights." Demanding your rights always gives you something to be frustrated about. Let the Lord manage what you get, and you can rest. Grappling for your rights, when you have little or no power, is a source for unforgiveness.

YOUR HEALING

God has something special for you. Are you more concerned about what the offender did to you than you are about the deficits in your relationship with your Father? If you are the offender, are you more concerned about what you did and what people think of you than your relationship with the Father? If you are, your focus is wrong. Until you receive a straight course from Him, you will continue suffering. God has something so much better for you. Go before Him and ask Him to speak to you about your walk with Him, and choose to be obedient to what He says.

To review this chapter, take a look at Galatians 6:1-9, and think about the four aspects of God's healing process. *Do not be deceived, God is not mocked; for whatever a man sows, this he* will also reap. *For the one who sows to his own flesh shall from the flesh reap corruption, but the one who sows to the Spirit shall from the Spirit reap eternal life. And let us not lose heart in doing good, for in due time we shall reap if we do not grow weary.*

Check your heart attitude. Where are you sowing—after the flesh or after the Spirit? Do you have unreconciled relationships because you are more interested in your own agenda? Are you functioning as god of your own life? In all things, is the supernatural life of Christ being exhibited in your life? You are called to walk humbly. Keep in mind, this forgiveness process is not about you, it is about the Lord Jesus Christ <u>in</u> you. Get your focus off yourself if you want to experience freedom in Christ.

Understand the damage. You reap what you sow. Do you understand the damage caused from sowing unrighteous seeds? Admit when you sow to the flesh and accept the consequences. Accept God's mighty work in whatever the consequences are and don't try to change them. Don't demand that the other person change whatsoever. Don't expect them to trust you. Damage has occurred and rebuilding trust may be a long, slow process.

Assess the resources for healing. Healing comes only as you sow after the Spirit. Have you sowed seeds of corruption? Start sowing seeds of righteousness by repenting. The ultimate resource is the perfect, holy, supernatural life of Jesus Christ. He gives you promises, and in Him all the promises are yes and amen. His promises are a resource, draw upon them. For example, Galatians 2:20 says, *I have been crucified with Christ; and it is no longer I who live, but Christ lives in me; and the life which I now live in the flesh I live by faith in the Son of God, who loved me, and delivered Himself up for me.* You are promised life in Jesus Christ. What other resource do you need?

You must take responsibility, though. You sowed the seeds, so faithfully harvest them. Don't pass blame on to someone else, regardless of their actions and attitudes.

Start the healing process. Don't lose heart in any circumstance. Sow faithfully after the Spirit because Galatians 6:9 promises that you will reap eternal life if you do not lose heart.

Finally, remember that this is a work that is <u>impossible</u> apart from the supernatural work of God. You cannot reconcile a relationship without the life of Christ being lived out in daily experience. So, seek the Lord, be obedient, and leave the results up to the Lord. His plans are better than yours anyway.

The Freedom to Love and Live Again

Summary of Chapter Ten

1. Our heart attitude must be right before the Lord in order to experience total restoration of relationships.
2. We must understand the damage that was done, whether we did the damage or received it.
3. The Lord provides endless resources in the healing process.
4. It is helpful to know the Lord's promises, and essential to fulfill my responsibilities in order to be fully rebuilt.
5. God has something good in store for us. He desires total and complete healing, and His life makes that possible.

Chapter Eleven

There __Is__ Freedom to Love and Live Again After Forgiveness

(Story told by Sandra)

If a friend of yours came to you and told you one of the stories that you have read in this book, as if that hurt and anguish had happened to them, you might not be surprised to hear your friend say that she was angry and bitter. We all have "reasons" why we might want to feel hurt and misused. But what does feeling that way really do for you? Is it helping you? Is it making you feel happier, stronger, more loved? Or is it just wearing you down, eating away from the inside out? Wouldn't it be nice to be free again?

Think about the hurts and abuses you read in this book and then focus on how these people feel today. John is free to love and live again after the abuse from his father. LuAnn is free to love and live again after forgiving Rocky for his unfaithfulness. Lisa is free to love and live again after being raped. Mark and his family are free to love and live again in rebuilt relationships. They all found freedom in forgiveness, God's merciful forgiveness of them, that allowed them to give and seek forgiveness, and rebuild broken relationships. Are you free to love and live again despite the past and present circumstances of your life?

Through the power of our Lord Jesus Christ, all of us are free to love and live again. But perhaps the most vivid example of a person finding freedom in forgiveness is one of our staff members, Sandra. Here is her story, in her words:

When I was four years old, a little boy threw a can of gasoline into a fire. I happened to be standing on the other side. The gas went through the fire and exploded up into my face, causing first, second, and third degree burns. I was left with thick, ugly scars requiring many plastic and reconstructive surgeries. Hundreds of times I asked myself: "Why did this happen to me? Who was to blame? Where was my mom, and why wasn't she watching me? Was it the little boy's fault that threw the gasoline? Was it my fault? Did I deserve it?"

When I looked into a mirror all I saw was scars.

As a young girl, I created a secret dream: that my doctors would make me beautiful! Everyone told me they would, and on television people came out of surgery looking beautiful. While growing up I had surgeries every summer, but I didn't see my dream coming true. On top of that my mother always left the room when the nurses came in to give me a shot or to change bandages. I was terrified and felt abandoned. It seemed when I really needed her the most she was gone.

Meanwhile, my dad was an alcoholic and was verbally and physically abusive. I can't remember the word "love" being spoken or any act of love being demonstrated by my parents. There was only fighting and turmoil in our home. However, an elderly man next door bought me treats and made me things from wood. But there was a price to pay. He showed me pornographic magazines and fondled and molested me over and over again.

School was very difficult for me also. Children reminded me daily that I "looked different." Because of the scars, I must have frightened some of them. I found it hard to concentrate on school work, and it seemed that nothing I did was ever good enough. I began trying to get approval and acceptance other ways.

While walking home from the show one night when I was 12, I was persuaded to get into a car with four men. They took me to a trailer and raped me repeatedly. Even though I felt dirty and empty inside, I thought someone at least wanted me for something. I wanted so desperately to love and be loved.

To escape the abuse of my father, I got pregnant and married at 15. I had my daughter, Pamela. That marriage lasted only one year. I divorced and married again at 17 to a man who was in the Air Force and lived in Japan. I thought I could get away from all my problems in Japan, but they followed me. My son, Dwayne, was born there, and within two years I left my husband and came back to Arizona, giving up my son to be raised by his father. I felt totally incapable of raising Dwayne at the time.

There Is Freedom to Love and Live Again After Forgiveness

Meanwhile, my parents had been divorced while I was in Japan, so I moved in with my mother. I began filling my loneliness with sexual relationships. By the time I was 25, I had been married four times. The longest marriage lasted less than two years.

My heart became hard and bitter and full of hatred, which began to eat me from the inside out. I became anorexic, then bulimic, and I had chronic migraine headaches, ulcers, a hysterectomy, mastectomies and many other major surgeries. I was in and out of doctors' offices and hospitals, constantly looking for a remedy for what was going on inside of me.

I also continued to look for doctors who said they could remove the scars on my face. To fight depression I tried alcohol, drugs, sexual relationships and even suicide, attempting to get fee from "me." I tried working many different jobs, but by 34 years of age, life seemed pretty meaningless and hopeless. I used to say:

I'm not me.
I'm not what you see.
I'm in a shell,
And it feels like hell.

I don't laugh.
I don't run.
I don't have fun.

I want out.
I want Free.
I want to be me.

Like John, Sandra had every human "reason" to live in bondage because of the abuse of others. Like Lisa, she had every human "reason" to be mad at God for allowing traumatic problems to disrupt her life. But like each of the people you have read about, Sandra chose to love and live again through the power of forgiveness. Sandra and others discovered a very important key to life: God's grace and forgiveness towards us are incomparable, therefore, we are able to love others by extending that same grace and forgiveness!

The Freedom to Love and Live Again

I first met Sandra at a *Victorious Christian Living Conference* that our ministry conducted. We taught about godship, man trying be the god of his own life. We taught about rejection, which was evident in Sandra's life. We taught about problems and how God, in His sovereignty, allows all kinds of circumstances in our life in order to conform us to the image of Jesus and to keep us dependent on Him. We taught the truth about who God is, who He has created us to be, and His unimaginable love for us. Then, we taught about reconciliation: God's forgiveness of us, giving forgiveness, seeking forgiveness and rebuilding relationships. This caught Sandra's attention.

Sandra realized she did not have the power to live in the kind of freedom she had just heard about. But she wanted that power. Several days later, on her knees in my office, Sandra repented of her sins and accepted Jesus as her Savior and Lord. She was empowered! She had new life! She was forgiven, and could now give and seek forgiveness from others and rebuild broken relationships.

As God began to reveal Himself to me through His word, He was teaching me how much He loved me and telling me that I needed to love others. **This is My commandment, that you love one another, just as I have loved you. Greater love has no one than this, that one lay down his life for his friends. You are My friends, if you do what I command you. This I command you, that you love one another** *(John 15:12-14, 17).*

I asked God "Who are my friends? Was that little boy who threw the can of gas in the fire my friend? Am I supposed to love him? Were my plastic surgeons my friends?" I didn't think I looked any better, and my dream of being beautiful hadn't come true. "And God, what about you? How come you let this happen to me?" I believed that my burns and surgeries caused my father to hate me and to drink too much. "All those other people who called me names, am I to love them too?"

Then God showed me Psalm 139:14a, 16: **I am fearfully and wonderfully made; Thine eyes have seen my unformed substance; and in Thy book they were all written, the days that were ordained for me, when as yet there was not one of them.** *I realized that if God already knew that all this was going to happen to me, there* *must be a purpose for it, and since God ordained it, it must be for good.*

Sandra, like Lisa in Chapter Seven, realized God's sovereignty in allowing difficult circumstances in her life. Absolutely nothing in life happens by accident. Nothing happens outside God's ability to change it if He desires. Yet, He allows it all for our good! Sandra learned that the answer lies not in <u>being</u> beautiful, but in <u>being</u> in Christ. In fact, life in Christ is greater than all the things that brought her there. Paul says, in Philippians 3:8, *More than that, I count all things to be loss in view of the surpassing value of knowing Christ Jesus my Lord, for whom I have suffered the loss of all things, and count them but rubbish in order that I may gain Christ.* Sandra counted beauty, proper treatment and reputation as losses, so that she could view the surpassing value of knowing Christ Jesus! Life's problems pale in comparison to the value of knowing the Lord Jesus Christ.

That realization enabled her to love those whom had abused her by <u>giving</u> them her forgiveness, just as Christ had forgiven her.

Ephesians 4:31-32 says, **Let all bitterness and wrath and anger and clamor and slander be put away from you, along with all malice. And be kind to one another, tender-hearted, forgiving each other, just as God in Christ also has forgiven you.** *As God brought people to mind, I began to forgive. I started with the little boy who threw the can of gas. I went to God and clearly identified all the hurt and the repercussions from the accident. I forgave that little boy and no longer held him guilty.*

Then the Lord brought my doctor to mind. I remembered the last time I had seen him. I had displayed an offensive and resentful attitude, because I blamed him for not fulfilling my dream of becoming beautiful. As I gave up my dream and accepted myself for who God made me to be, I realized that I also needed to accept my doctor and I wondered if he still accepted me. **If... you remember that your brother has something against you... go ... be reconciled to your brother.** *(Matthew 5:23)*

I knew that God wanted me to seek forgiveness from my doctor. So, I first went to God, confessing my sin, and then to my doctor. I admitted that my actions and attitudes were wrong and humbly asked him for forgiveness. As he forgave me, the chains of sin were broken and I was FREE!

While I was in the doctor's office, he showed me slides of my burns and each of my surgeries as I was growing up. I had never seen them before, and for the first time I realized what my parents must have gone through. They must have had tremendous pain and guilt, feelings of frustration, anger, helplessness and hopelessness. Before, I had only thought about my own pain.

I knew that I needed to go to my mother and seek her forgiveness. While praying and confessing my sin to the Lord, He revealed the truth of my attitudes towards my mother. All those years I had been taking from her and, in a way, I was trying to make her pay for what had happened to me. As I asked her to forgive me, I shared with her how God, as sovereign over all things, had allowed this to happen to me. At that very moment my mother became free from the guilt she had carried for over 30 years. She had received freedom in my asking for forgiveness, and I received a blessing. Our relationship has grown closer ever since.

Then, the Lord gave me the desire to find my Dad whom I hadn't seen in over 12 years. Exodus 20:12a says, **Honor your father and your mother.** In the past I had been filled with hatred, resentment, and bitterness and I fought depression constantly. I hated him for the beatings, the abandonment, his alcoholic rages and his mental torment. I did not know what honoring him would look like.

But the Lord gave me a vision. In that vision I saw my Savior on the cross, between my dad and me. I saw a shadow of the cross rather than my needy father. I wanted that to be real, not only a vision. The Lord revealed to me that the things that my father did were no different than what I did! He reacted out of alcoholism; I reacted out of my own anger. God's forgiveness of me made it possible for me to forgive my Dad.

I knew I had to find my Dad, for God had not made a mistake in giving him to me as my father. I found him in a tavern. He was shocked to see me and hardly knew me. I was a little shocked, too! He looked old and very skinny. The alcohol had caught up with him, and he still had a foul mouth. But, by God's grace, I could love him in spite of his words. I continued to visit him for years after that, and I sought forgiveness from him for my actions and attitudes that did not honor him, and I shared my new life with him.

One night while visiting him in the hospital, I had the privilege of hearing him pray to receive the Lord Jesus Christ into his life. Now Christ on the cross didn't have to stand between my father and me any more. Instead, we were joined together in love. God changed hate into love! I couldn't hold my father guilty any more.

The more convinced I became that God had not made a mistake in giving him to me as a father, the more I loved him. Two years later, my Dad died, but I know I'll see him again. He's _free_!

I continued to pray to the Lord about my family and He put on my heart the desire to seek my children's forgiveness. Even though my daughter, Pamela, had prayed to receive Christ shortly after I did, she disappeared from my life and from the lives of her first husband and two children. No one knew her whereabouts for 2 1/2 years. Although my heart was breaking, I released Pam to the Lord, and prayed for a revival in her heart.

God apprehended Pam's heart and brought her to a truth-filled relationship with Himself. Pam actually initiated contact with me and asked my forgiveness for some very specific actions she had taken. That opened a door for a great deal of mutual reconciliation, and not only did I have a prodigal daughter returned to me, I had a beautiful relationship with a dear "sister-in-the-Lord." God restored our relationship and bonded our hearts with deeper love and total acceptance for one another.

Nine months later, just prior to Pam's 31st birthday, she was returning from a doctor's appointment with her daughter, Montana. Without cause, her heart stopped and she fell to the kitchen floor and died. Our lives are very fragile and temporary, so it is important to make things right with everyone immediately. I have spent many hours helping my son-in-law understand the sovereign purposes of God in all this.

Years before seeking forgiveness from Pam, I had been led to contact my son, Dwayne, after a seventeen-year separation to ask his forgiveness. Miraculously, it seemed, Dwayne flew from Denver to meet with me. God blessed our meeting with a heartfelt reconciliation. I also went to Dwayne's father, (my former husband), and sought his forgiveness for the hurt I had caused him and for my wrong actions during our marriage and divorce. When my son was married in Denver, his father and stepmother paid for my airfare and hotel accommodations so that I could attend the ceremony. We all stood together as his parents. We remain friends and get together when possible. <u>Forgiveness</u> has set us <u>free</u>. **Forgiving each other, whoever has a complaint against anyone just as the Lord forgave you, so also should you** (Ephesians 4:32).

After asking for forgiveness from my son's father, I thought of all the other relationships I had had. I made a list as the Holy Spirit brought them to mind, and after forgiving any hurt, I proceeded to contact each person by phone. The process took weeks, but I whittled my list down to four people, who I was unable to locate. I prayed to the Lord, agreeing that if He would bring them into my life, I would seek their forgiveness.

The Lord is faithful to complete His good work. I met one of the four at a high school reunion. Another, whom I had not seen for 14 years, got my phone number from my mother and called me. And one of my former husbands whom I had not seen in 27 years called when he saw his last name in the phone book while traveling through Phoenix. We met for dinner and not only did I seek his forgiveness, but he also asked for mine! I will not be surprised as to how the Lord will bring the last person on my list into my life for forgiveness. **For I am confident of this very thing, that He who began a good work in you will perfect it until the day of Christ Jesus** (Philippians 1:6).

After a very difficult childhood, Sandra tried to live life according to her own ways. That produced nothing but more heartache. She created for herself many problems that could have been avoided. But, in the Lord's grace and mercy, her sin was revealed and she repented of each of the ways she had tried to be god of her own life.

Sandra also realized, just as Lisa in Chapter Seven did, that God called her to love others, including those who hurt her. That love is supernatural, and its only source is God Himself! One cannot give what one does not have! Love of others will result in freely forgiving them as Christ has forgiven you. True forgiveness is not possible without Christ.

What was done to make restoration possible between Mark and his family, John and his dad, Lisa and her boyfriend, and Sandra and her family? Simply the supernatural love of the Lord Jesus Christ being poured out through each of them. *In this is love, not that we loved God, but that He loved us and sent His Son to be the Propitiation for our sins. Beloved, if God so loved us, we also ought to love one another* (1 John 4:10-11). This is not a love that can be conjured up from within. To borrow an anonymous expression, "It is the reckless, raging fury that is the love of God."

Sandra now lives on faith, ministering God's supernatural truth to others through our discipleship training center. When a person truly experiences the freedom of forgiveness and lives a life reflective of the almighty love of Jesus Christ, they cannot help but "pour out" the experience to others. In turn, others begin to "pour out" to the next generation. Here is an example of Sandra's discipleship:

My mom had a friend, Peter, to whom I looked up, as a father figure. He was a very bitter, angry man who never talked about his family. Before I met Christ I was bitter too, so we hit it off really well.

Several years later, after I accepted Christ and began to allow the life of Christ to be lived out in me, I bought Peter a book entitled, <u>A Man Called Peter</u>. For the first time, I saw Peter show emotion. That was only a small doorway to what would follow later.

He was a brilliant man, and I often felt intimidated by him. He also did not readily accept God's call in my life to ministry. "You are nothing but a high class beggar," he told me. He also made sarcastic comments when the things of God were mentioned. However, he constantly evaluated my life.

Later, he got cancer and was placed in hospice care where Mom and I visited him regularly. He went downhill medically and the Lord impressed upon me to share the Gospel with him one day. Peter met Jesus while lying in a hospice bed! I knew how hard his heart had been, so I asked the Lord to give me confirmation that Peter really had turned his life over to Him. When I went in the next day, I got confirmation. With his hands to his chest, Peter said, "Something is all different inside." He was also telling all the nurses, doctors, and others who entered his room about Jesus!

Peter had left his wife pregnant with their third child about 40 years earlier, and had only recently found out that he had three daughters instead of two. In the days that followed his salvation, he contacted each of his three daughters and asked their forgiveness for not being the father he needed to be! The Lord used my own experiences of reconciliation with my family to prompt Peter to do the same!

For hours, while Peter lay in a comatose state, I pressed my hand to his chest, anticipating his last heartbeat. Suddenly, I asked, "Peter, do you see Jesus?" His eyes popped wide open, and he opened his mouth to speak. No words came forth, but the peace on his face was more obvious than any "yes" he could have spoken. Three weeks after Peter joined the Royal Family he went home to be with Jesus, reconciled to God and to his daughters.

Sandra has "seen the vision" and lives out the verses that our ministry uses as our theme: *The Spirit of the Lord God is upon me, because the Lord has anointed me to bring good news to the afflicted; He has sent me to bind up the brokenhearted, to proclaim liberty to captives, and freedom to prisoners.* (Isaiah 61:1-3)

THERE IS FREEDOM IN THE LORD JESUS CHRIST
TO LOVE AND LIVE AGAIN!

Summary of Chapter Eleven

1. Being god of one's own life brings only death and destruction.
2. Playing god makes it necessary to confess to the Lord and repent of sin.
3. Problems in life are a vehicle the Lord uses to conform each of us to the image of Jesus Christ.
4. New life in Christ is greater than things that bring us to Christ. In fact, problems pale in comparison to the glory of God.
5. True forgiveness is not possible without Christ.
6. Restoration of relationships happens as others are loved and accepted as Christ loves and accepts us.

The Freedom to Love and Live Again

VCL International
MISSION STATEMENT

VCL International is a nondenominational biblical discipleship training ministry. It is committed to renewal and discipleship in the body of Christ. VCL International is a total-life ministry. Our purpose is to see new life in Christ become the daily living experience of each individual and family to whom we minister. Our source book is the Bible, the Word of the living God, in which knowledge of God, salvation in Jesus Christ, and directions for effective living are found.

Biblical principles are diligently taught in discipleship, through the enabling power of the Holy Spirit. The goal is to teach individuals how to live and stand complete in Christ, fully equipped by His life and Word, with the ability to reproduce in the lives of others.

VCL International believes that only the appropriating and living of Christ's life produces genuine renewal for the individual, the family, and the church.

Fold One—We are committed to providing biblical discipleship to those seeking help. This provision is both the initial and the ultimate "product" of VCL International.

Fold Two—The continuous recruiting and training of biblical disciples is essential for expanding biblical discipleship beyond what can be provided by existing VCLI personnel.

Fold Three—The primary purpose for training biblical discipleship personnel is to enable us to establish centers (both VCL International centers and ministries in local church bodies) which will function to (1) provide biblical discipleship and (2) train biblical disciples.

Level I
VICTORIOUS CHRISTIAN LIVING CONFERENCE

Are you experiencing abundant life? Jesus said, "I came that you might have life and have it abundantly" (John 10:10). There is no circumstance or relationship that can stand in the way of having an abundant life. We call this abundant life **Victorious Christian Living**. The VCL Conference will show you how this abundant life can be yours.

Victorious Christian Living is possible:
* As you overcome the one thing that keeps you from living victoriously.
* As God sets you free from the feelings of rejection and insecurity.
* As you learn to keep circumstances from controlling you.
* As you learn that problems can work for your benefit.
* As you understand the destructiveness of selfishness and how to stop it.
* As you change the direction of your life for the better.
* As you become confident in Christ.
* As you accept your true righteousness in Christ and gain fulfillment.
* As you experience complete healing from your past through true forgiveness.
* As you learn to be at peace in the midst of a "stress-filled" world.
* As you learn to let God's love flow through you to others.

Level 2
LIFE MINISTRY TRAINING

This training course is approximately 40 hours. These sessions are designed to help people fully understand and communicate the Victorious Christian Living lessons to others. The sessions include teaching and practical application. The instruction is reinforced by actual ministry experience. Each person is given a ministry partner. The objective is to develop confidence in Christians by giving them tools and a workable understanding of biblical principles for addressing the basic problems of living. Class members receive the valuable Life Ministry Manual and are shown how to use it to minister to others.

Life Ministry Training will teach you:
* How to stand against the fear of discipling others.
* How to minister to others using the messages learned from the Victorious Christian Living Conference.
* How to establish and conduct a VCL Conference Group.
* How to minister to troubled marriages.
* How to equip parents in training up their children in the ways of the Lord.

Level 3
SEVEN AREAS OF LIFE TRAINING

S. A. L.T. is our third level of training. In this level of training you receive a copy of the **Biblical Resource Manual**. It is a wealth of material designed to train someone in the disciplining process. It contains 49 modules covering the <u>seven areas of life</u> as seen in Scripture. These seven areas are:

1. Spiritual—our relationship with God.
2. Psychological—our relationship with our mind, will and emotions, our soul.
3. Social—our relationship with other people.
4. Physical—our relationship with our body.
5. Financial—our relationship with our job and money in general.
6. Marital—our relationship with our spouse.
7. Parental—our relationship with our children.

Each area of life includes the <u>seven requirements for Godly living</u>. They are:

1. Repentance
2. Identification Truth
3. Disciplines
4. Obedience
5. Fruit of the Spirit
6. Victory
7. Vision

One of these modules will be covered each week. This provides an ongoing system of training.

Order Form

	Price	Quantity	Total
Victorious Christian Living Conference			
Pkg. A:1 Manual and 1 Audio Set	$100 x	_____	= _____
Pkg. B:1 Manual and 1 Audio Set	$150 x	_____	= _____
Additional Manual	$ 50 x	_____	= _____
Video Set	$100 x	_____	= _____
Leader's Guide	$ 25 x	_____	= _____
Transparencies			
Small format (2 diagrams/pg.)	$100 x	_____	= _____
Large format (1 diagram/pg.)	$150 x	_____	= _____
Life Ministry Training			
Life Ministry Manual	$ 60 x	_____	= _____
LMT Training Notebook	$ 15 x	_____	= _____
LMT Training Video Set	$395 x	_____	= _____
LMT Training Director's Manual	$ 75 x	_____	= _____
Seven Areas of Life Training			
Biblical Discipleship Resource	$ 75 x	_____	= _____
Pastors' Information			
Ministry Explanation	$ 2.^{50} x	_____	= _____
Total			_____

Prices subject to change without notice.

Please make all checks in U.S. $ to **VCL International**

Mail to: VCL International
14819 N. Cave Creek Rd.
Phoenix, AZ 85032
1-888-577-4904